TIPPING THE SCALES

How to fight back against life-threatening or quality of life threatening diseases - a manual for patients, carers and health professionals

Dr. Sean Collins, B.A. (Psych.), D.C.H.

Tipping the Scales

This manual is published by Ardagh Clinic/NICABM (Ireland)
118 Stillorgan Rd, Dublin 4, Co. Dublin. Tel: 01-260 0118

1st October 1997

The recommendations made in this book are generic and are not meant to replace formal medical or psychiatric treatment. Individuals with medical problems should consult with their physicians about the appropriateness of following any programme and discuss appropriate modifications relevant to their unique circumstances and condition.

Not for Profit: Net profits from the sale of this manual in Ireland in 1997/'98 will go to fund research and training in the field of behavioural medicine in 1997/'98.

This book describes a programme for fighting back against serious illness and is published by the Ardagh Clinic/ NICABM (Ireland) to coincide with a radio series of the same name being broadcast by Radio Telefis Eireann Sept-Dec 1997. The content does not reflect the position or policy of RTE and no official endorsement by RTE of the content should be inferred.

ISBN : 0-9521444-3-3
1. Health 2. Psychology 3. Mind and body 4 Holistic health

Printed in Dublin by DigiSource Limited
Cover design, layout, & additional material: Rhoda Draper
Yoga Illustrations by Hugh Collins

Omega Plus

Interstellar particle
wandering
away, away
no itinerary planned
perhaps to pass the Milky Way
perhaps beyond
to Andromedean suburbs
and sympathetic nebulae.
Wandering, just wandering
away, away
through space eternal tomb.
no itinerary
save take heed
of time imprisoned womb.

Geraldine Meyler (1950-1995)

(Authors note: Three days before she died from cancer in 1995, at age 45, Geraldine Meyler, spent almost an hour debating Hawking's concepts of space and time with me. An exceptional, intelligent, and courageous woman, her belief in human magnificence and potential inspired parts of the research paralleling this book which is dedicated to her memory.)

Acknowledgements

I wish to thank:

Rhoda Draper, my co-conspirator, pal, researcher and editor, without whom this book would never have happened

Teri Garvey for believing in human possibilities and the concepts of psychoneuroimmunology

Dr. Andrea Kingston, my medical mentor and friend

My brother Michael Collins (1944 - 1989) for believing in me

Valerie Collins, without whom I would not have survived my original heart attack

The authors in this field who inspire us all

My clients who are really my teachers

My students who are also my teachers

My teachers who motivated and inspired me

The doctors and surgeons who saved me, for their knowledge and skill

Contents

Preface

In the early 60's I was seriously ill with Hodgkin`s disease (cancer of the lymphatic system). Thirty years later, I feel that the factors which helped me beat the disease included not only the conventional treatments of surgery and radiation but also the acceptance, by the medical consultant, of my involvement in my recovery and by his optimistic attitude towards my future plans.

My 'involvement' in my recovery was an instinctive, intuitive change of diet and my plans were the optimistic plans of any teenager, but the acceptance of these two factors by the "expert" was hugely important to me then.

Over the thirty years since, my instinctive and intuitive feelings about 'complementary' therapies have deepened, and have resolved into three specific and significant areas. Firstly, that the mind, as expressed in an optimistic attitude, has a huge effect on healing. Secondly, that complementary therapies, especially in the areas of diet, herbs, homoeopathy and hypnosis, are extremely important along with conventional medical practice. Finally, that any patient needs to feel involved in the management of their illness and recovery, and to have this involvement accepted by their medical team.

These three areas were vital to me when I again faced cancer in 1995 and helped me, I feel, to tip the scales in my favour. These three areas are now in the forefront of medical research, in the science known as PNI or psychoneuroimmunology. Their day has come. They appear not just in the 'alternative' health magazines but in the mainstream medical journals. They have gone from being 'flaky fringe' to being at the forefront of medical and scientific research.

Just how much at the forefront they were, I was to find out when I began working with Dr. Sean Collins on the current radio series *'Tipping the Scales'*. I confined my interviews to medically qualified doctors and consultants and, far from having a scarcity of interviewees in this area of PNI , my difficulty was just how to fit in all the interested parties. As I said in early programmes in the series, this is not a new age idea from California but rather an idea and area of study which has been here for over seventy years and was expressed most recently in a Mind-Body Medicine conference organised, earlier this year, by Prof. Fergus Shanahan of Cork University Hospital. Chief among the interested parties in *Tipping the scales* was, of course, Dr. Sean Collins, the series consultant. Having worked with him on Radio 1, since 1996, on series such as *The ABC; the Anti-Blank Course*, a series on performance anxiety for students, and on *PS: Practical strategies for taking charge of your life,* I knew of his skills as a therapist and researcher in the general areas of psychology and hypnotherapy. Working on *Tipping the Scales*, I got to see the range of his involvement in the area of psychoneuroimmunology, from the five hundred or so books and articles he has read, on the subject, to the conferences he has attended, to the pilot research programme he has organised.

This is not the book of the series but, rather, a book which goes with the series. I feel its practical down to earth approach, backed by the depth of research gone into it, and by the skills of Sean Collins as a therapist and coach, will make it invaluable for anybody who is, in Sean's words, 'life -challenged'.

For anybody facing a serious illness and involvement with a medical team it will be an essential item in their armoury of "fighting back" tools - one which should help them to tip the scales to wellness and health.

I wish it and them every success.

Teri Garvey

Foreword

As medical knowledge has advanced in the last thirty years or so, it has become increasingly clear that more and more illness, especially in the developed world, is caused by our behaviour. Our drinking, eating and smoking habits can all influence our chances of developing illnesses such as cancer, stroke and heart disease.

Much of this knowledge about the link between behaviour and illness has been freely available in the media, of course. It must be a small minority of people, for instance, who are not aware that smoking causes lung cancer and that eating a lot of animal fat can give cholesterol levels high enough to cause ischaemic heart disease.

What is emerging through recent research, however, is the intriguing possibility that our internal world, our feelings and emotions, may also play a *causal* role in physical illness. And whilst we know, for example, that stress levels may precipitate a heart attack in some individuals, the idea that our mental state could affect our immune system, leaving us *vulnerable* to a variety of illnesses, is revolutionary, and raises a bewildering number of issues and possibilities for patients and their doctors.

If we suppose it is true, however, that negative emotions and behaviours can influence health for the worse, it must surely be possible for the right changes of behaviour and thinking style to create well-being and allow improvement of, or even cure of, an illness... if we can only find out what the right changes are.

In the UK, the medical profession are largely sceptical about the effects of behavioural change on illness and many dismiss it as close to witchcraft. This is probably because some of the studies that have been done have not always used rigorous scientific method, plus the fact that most of the research has been done in the USA, rather than on home territory, and is therefore less well known. Time pressure and rapid developments within conventional medicine, as always, also work against physicians' learning about behavioural techniques.

However, some doctors, like myself, are willing to accept this link between mind and body and are open to the intriguing possibilities which Behavioural Medicine then holds for us. It stands to reason that these techniques give hope to the patients we see, encourage them to participate in their care in a way which complements conventional treatment. This can only improve the person's quality of life and their relationships with their carers, professional and otherwise.

When I tell someone that they have a serious illness such as cancer, initially there may be a whole range of reactions, even within the same person, from complete denial, through anger and despair to depression The person receiving the information often becomes particularly vulnerable, and information given inappropriately at this time, can be incredibly demotivating, possibly even *life-shortening*. (Unfortunately, we do not always get it right and it is a skilled doctor who is always able to provide the correct amount of information, in the correct way and at the correct time for each individual.)

Some people, however, react very positively and with determination, seeing a health crisis much more as a chance to review what is happening in their lives and to consider a change of direction. In other words, such a crisis can motivate a person wonderfully. There is often a special openness as well, to new ideas and to taking advice; a window of opportunity is created.

It is precisely at this time, and for these people, that Sean Collins' book is likely to be most useful and most influential in tipping the balance towards recovery and good health. Within these pages is presented a summary of the very best techniques for change currently available and where available, the evidence for their use; if the right changes are anywhere, they are here.

I hope that as many doctors as patients will read this book and that it will come into common usage within the medical profession, both in the UK and in Ireland, as part of a standard range of options for patients when they are first told they have a life-challenging illness. In its current form it truly compliments medical treatment and will provide a focus for discussion between patient and doctor which can only result in both being better informed and thus in better care.

It is the *'how to'* for developing a positive attitude if you have a serious condition. More than that, though, there are lessons within it for all of us to improve our quality of life, our awareness and to keep us healthy for longer.

Andrea Kingston, MB ChB MRCGP
General Practitioner

Prologue

(Personal)

Wednesday, 5th July 1950
Born to Eileen Collins (nee Suttle) and Patrick (Pat) Collins, a boy Sean Anthony....

Friday, 1st July 1955
I'll be five next week... Uncle John, Mammy's brother is dead... from a heart attack... what's that? .... What does dead mean.... do all men die at 40 or 50? .... Might my Daddy die?

November, 1955
A little boy sitting at the top of the stairs... listening... parents are talking... "There's a baby coming..." How do they know when? .... "There may be problems... risk of thrombosis!" What's thrombosis... a musical instrument? ...

Saturday, 14th July 1956
Olivia, my little baby sister has been born... is this Uncle John coming back? Is this what dying is? The person gets born into another body… what a great idea!

Years of Mammy being sick... Doctor Daly in the middle of the night... a kind man... even came once in slippers and dressing gown! Every week-end seemed to be fight time between Mum and Dad... were other families like this, did their parents fight too? Yet we went to Mass a lot... didn't do it there! Was this what heart disease does to you... makes you moody and cranky? Did that moodiness flow to everyone else? God, its hard... being a little boy!

Hey! I found a frog in Cuddy's field to-day and brought it home... boy can it hop! ..... Mammy jumping onto a chair in the front room... hey this is fun ... she's scared of it! Next day... Mammy has to go into hospital .... coronary thrombosis ... God I did that! I hurt my Mammy... what sort of person am I? Guilt ... nobody to talk to! Look grown up ... you're a big boy now... big boys don't cry .... don't upset your mother!

June, 1960
A sunny morning… Mum and Dad have been fighting .... Mum's very upset. I have to 'fix' this! I know - get her a present... yes, that'll make things right! Sneaking my money box out to the back shed... get the big kitchen knife... rattle the money out of the box...

off down to Oliver Carthy's shop on Drumcondra Road, little sister in tow. Aha! A little yellow brooch... the very thing... my Mammy will be happy! Back to the house... explosive anger! ... "Why did you waste money on rubbish like that?" ... Brooch thrown against the wall... broken in bits... confusion! Does she love me? ... Little sister upset... what does she understand? Is this what a heart condition does?

1961 - 1968 (the school years)
"Get your own lunch ..." "Don't upset your mother..." "Your Mother's resting..." Hospital... visits... smell of ether ... "Bring this grapefruit up to your Mammy..." Long shiny corridors... trying to be a "big boy" .. (tears as I write this) .

Saturday 15th June 1968 - 3.15 p.m.
Swimming at Bullock harbour with my pal Louis - a lovely sunny early Summer's day. It's wonderful to be alive (I'll be eighteen in three weeks!). Visited my Mum in the Bon Secours Hospital in Glasnevin this morning. Louis brought her a rose in a little blue glass vase; she liked it. She gave me a ten shilling note: "Don't spend it on you know what!" Cigarettes of course....

Sunday, 16th June 1968 - 07.10 a.m.
The phone is ringing! Who would be phoning at that hour? The clatter of my Dad's feet rushing down the stairs; just a few words, that's all... Then my bedroom door opening... my Dad's face... tears... I've never seen tears on his face before. "Mammy died last night." What does that mean? ...Corpus Christi Church for early Mass with Dad... walking down the steps after Mass, in the sunlight... holding my Dad's hand... big boys don't do that... but this is different... it's OK to-day. The birds are singing outside the church... why do they keep doing that? My Mammy is dead! The morgue... how small she looks! Is this what heart disease is?

Wednesday 14th June 1989 - 2.15 p.m.
Sunny California, East of Palm Springs, driving in the desert... sudden fierce pain in my chest... pull to the side of the road... what is it? Do some yoga breathing (from long ago)... take some pain killers... my phone won't work... panic! What is this pain in my chest? I never had anything like this before... please let it stop! Surf the waves of pain... nothing else I can do. My God, please let this stop! Eventually it abates... whew! I'm OK - must have been indigestion ... don't tell anyone! Next morning: it's back - the pain - not as bad... but it's there much of the time, particularly when I move about... don't tell anyone! Emergency medical centre: "you've had a heart attack." No, that can't be right... I'm only 38 years of age! Lots of tests... "You've got a blocked artery

and one substantially blocked... necrotic tissue in your heart muscle; you must have a bypass." "Will I die now?..." "No... but..." "Will I die next week?" " No, but... you are unlikely to last two years without a bypass." I won't accept that! Other opinions... same diagnosis, same prognosis... telling my wife modified versions of the truth... must protect people from the truth... now, very scared! That ache in the night... the next one... maybe the final one? Rush back to Ireland... Like ET, must phone home... home - that's where I'll be OK! Another opinion: "You've had a heart attack" ...Now I accept this as truth! "You're stable... take your tablets and see what happens."

Back to California... Change your lifestyle?... Walking... used to watch people walking on TV. First morning: walk to the gate ... that's enough... add one minute a day. Yoga, visualisation... vegetarian, then vegan... vitamin therapy... reading 1-2 books a week on heart disease... conflicting opinions... Pains in my chest as I walk... not enough oxygen getting to my heart muscle. Charts of the heart on the wall in my study... visualisation... a little diver swimming up through my arteries, hacking away at the plaque... at the blockages... every day. Lymph breathing... Mayr Cure detox programme... must offer my body and spirit an optimum healing environment... it already knows how to be well. God would never have limited miracles to those who could afford an air ticket to Lourdes... would He? Everyone has miracles available... don't they? Week by week, one minute more onto my walking regimen each day... the pain in my chest grows a little less each week. If it swims, walks, flies, or moves under its own steam, I don't eat it. Hey! It's Labor Day, and I walked for a half an hour without any chest pain! Yippee! ...Never take your eye off the ball! .... I've been one step ahead of the grim reaper .. but now I am really getting ahead.

Saturday 16th December 1989

Back to Ireland for Christmas... thoughts of Grafton Street... Bewleys... Christmas lights... family... my Dad... my surgeon brother hugging me at the airport... I don't remember him doing that before... A Christmas present of an angiogram... typical surgeon! Looking at my heart on the monitors... the rush of the radioactive dye squirting into my heart... "A little warm sensation..." says the cardiologist... "Aha! ...your left anterior descending artery's 100% blocked and your circumflex is 80% occluded... however, it appears your body has done its own bypass, and you now have adequate circulation around the blockage.".. Hey!... It's my own private miracle... in less than six months... by offering my body and spirit their very own *optimum healing environment.*

Martin Luther King said "I have a dream", and I also planted a dream into my future at the time. In December 1989, I created a picture in my mind that on the 1st July, 1990, I would sit down to breakfast with my family, at home in Anaheim, and have bacon, eggs, sausages and coffee, snap my fingers and say to myself "What heart attack?". I used that image, day after day after day, as I applied more than 20 different approaches in my in my quest for recovery.

Thursday, 27th June, 1990 - 3.30 p.m.

Sunny California... my beeper is buzzing... Oh my God, a 'Code 1'! ... I've never had one of those before... are the kids OK? ....Quick, ring home! ... Michael, my brother in San Diego can't be contacted... do I know where he might be? ...Rushing home ... secretary says "One car is in the garage and the other's out front, but there's no answer"... He's probably gone away for a few days. Yes, that's it! ... Ringing his house... again and again and again... "Please leave a message after the tone..." His voice over and over: "...please leave a message after the tone". Then ... the phone is answered... at last... relief ... it's him!... But no... a female voice: "Who is that?" I ask ... "Officer Cook of the San Diego Police department... please clear the line." "No!".... I reply .... "where's my brother?" ... "Who are you?" asks the voice ... "I'm Sean, Michael's brother. Where is he? Is he alright? Has he been hurt?" Evasive answers... "Please can you call back later?" ... "No!".........By now I'm shouting .....

"I'm sorry... your brother is deceased." I'm screaming... "Please don't let this be true! ...No! This can't be true! ...My lovely brother can't be dead! ... No!... No!... No! ...Please don't let this be true..." In my head, I plead, I negotiate, I...

The long drive to San Diego: Valerie driving... my mind in turmoil... am I going to be able to handle this... will my heart break . . or just stop? I had a heart attack less than twelve months ago... Can my damaged heart take this much pain? ...... Sending my brother home to Ireland in a casket... I can't handle this... my heart is broken! I'm still feeling the warmth of the hug he gave me last week-end. "...We think your brother died of a heart attack." ... A small brown envelope from the coroner's man... his wallet.. his keys... Is that all that's left of him? My God, he was so healthy... and he used to worry about *me!* ... All of this just five day before my 1st of July dream... had I wasted my time? Was I going to die anyway?

The months passing... slowly put myself back together... home to Ireland in September... my Dad devastated... my sisters and brother devastated... the price tag of heart disease... the distributions, the conflicts... back to America, but to prepare for returning to Ireland. Like ET, I needed to go 'home'!

March, 1991
Returned to Ireland... settled back to normality... my heart is fine and I stay healthy.

Monday, 24th February, 1997
(My diary) Started to-day with a significant attack of angina. This is a warning, I believe, to do something **now**. Weight: 14 stone 7 lbs.! Must get back on my programme! ... I've drifted seriously away from it...

Saturday, 8th March, 1997: 06.30 a.m.
I'm teaching to-day. God! I have a pain in my chest... and in my arms! Tell nobody! Ring Rhoda... "I've a bit of a bug... can't teach to-day... go to 'Plan B' (you teach for me!!)." Lie down... hope the pain will go... no point in going to the doctor on a Saturday! Do relaxation, deep breathing, take pain-killers ... the pain won't go! Evening comes... I feel very alone... a nights sleep will get rid of the pain. Sunday morning: pain is back in chest and arms... more tablets... more relaxation. Phone Rhoda again... "I can't teach... please fill in for me." Sunday 3.30 p.m: my brother is on the phone... "Uncle Liam has died in Clonakilty ... we're going to fly down for the removal this afternoon." Pain is there... but I'll go anyhow. Go to Dublin Airport... meet my brother and sister and their spouses... say nothing about the pain ... don't tell anyone! Attended the removal in Clonakilty... flew back that night... more pain... more tablets... still alone... I'm sure the pain will be gone in the morning...

Monday 10th march 1997 - 08.55 a.m.
Locking the front door... am I ever coming back? Fear... waiting for the doctor... ECG... "Go to hospital immediately... don't collect your toothbrush." Driving to St. Vincent's Hospital... a blur of admissions, phone calls, my diary, cancelling my life... tests... angiogram... cardiac incidents... oxygen... Blackrock Clinic... arguments... trying to keep control... photographs... angio film... blockages... "You need a bypass." "Can we defer?" "No! We can operate to-morrow, your heart has sustained no damage - we have a fresh surgical team and you're in reasonably good shape... or... we can wait, perhaps as long as two or three days... you may have a massive heart attack in the middle of the night, do damage... We can rush in - probably tired, having already operated that day - and then do our best to save you. It's your choice!"

More fear... am I going to die? What's it like to be dead? Being shaved... prepared for theatre... theatre? There's nothing theatrical or entertaining about an operation, so why call it a theatre...? **(To be continued)**

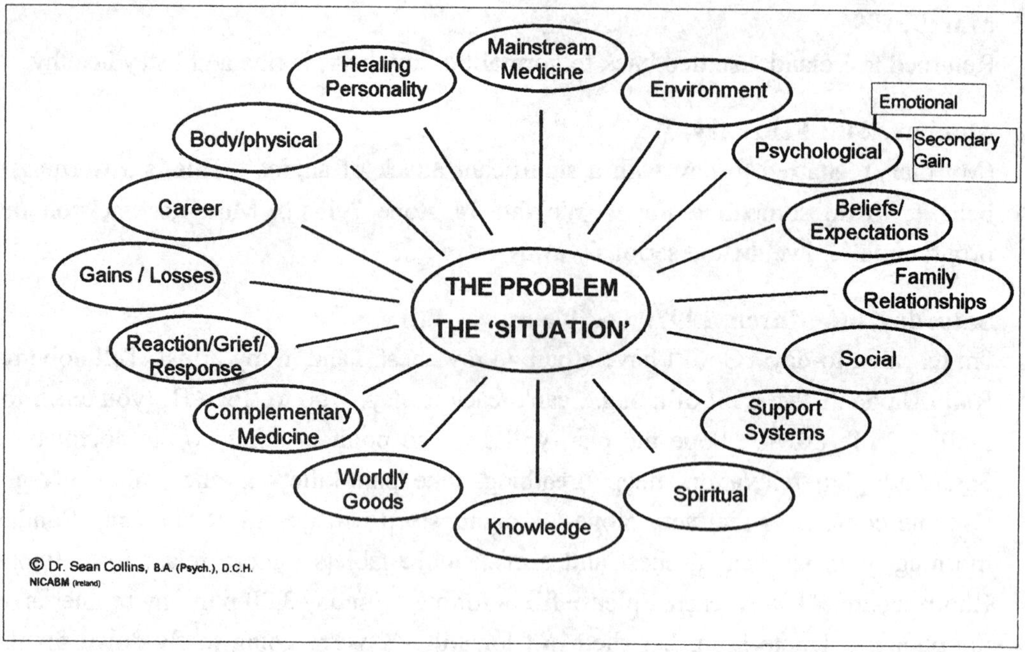

1. **The Problem**: *An overview of aspects of self & living - for immediate and* ***essential*** *review*

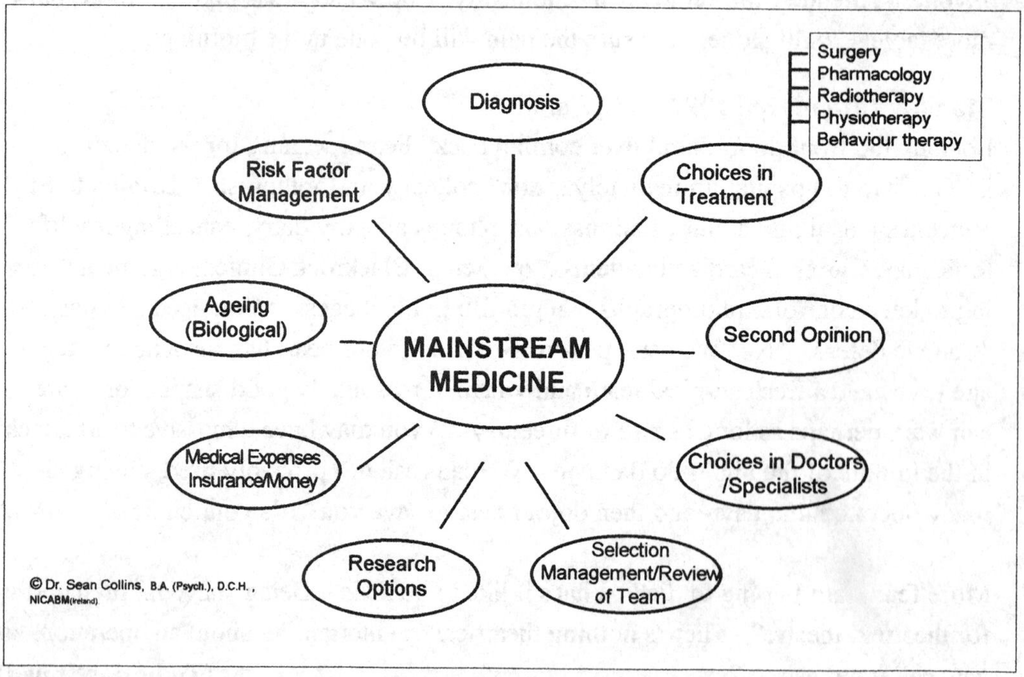

18. **Mainstream Medicine:** *Significant medical-related considerations*

Introduction

"When illness strikes suddenly, it's like hitting a wall at 60 m.p.h."

Until comparatively recently, it was largely believed that there was no mind-body connection, that there was nothing meaningful patients could do to affect the progression of their diseases. Many philosophers held, however, that the body could influence the mind! Then suddenly, within a few years of each other, came a number of ground-breaking or land-mark scientific studies showing that psychosocial intervention and behavioural change could lengthen life expectancy for certain terminal cancer sufferers, and open and clear arteries for people with advanced heart disease. Such research indicates that your **behaviour** and **how you think** and **react** have a significant influence on how well you will manage an illness and on whether you are likely to achieve a remission, a cure, or improve the quality of your life while living with the illness.

A very real and valid fear exists among doctors that preliminary findings in this area may prove dangerous to patients. Their concern is that these findings may encourage patients, not trained in assessing or interpreting preliminary data, to use them as a basis for rejecting conventional treatment. They also worry that patients might regard the findings as scientific proof that psychotherapy and other approaches offer an alternative cure for their disease, and therefore put themselves at risk by turning away from the more difficult avenues of treatment, such as chemotherapy, surgery, medication or radiation, which might offer them the best chance of recovery.

If I have a shrub in my garden that has been thriving and, in order to make way for some new plants, I move it to a shadier and maybe damper part of the garden where now it does poorly. I can prune this shrub. I can add chemicals. I can clear weeds, I can water it... but, am I addressing the real issue? These measures may help in the short term, but the real solution is to restore it to an appropriate environment in which it can thrive again. To my knowledge, there has never been a single doctor or physician in history who has ever been evaluated scientifically as having 'healed' anyone. Doctors are highly trained individuals with comprehensive knowledge of illness, disease, treatments and side effects. They have the necessary skills to diagnose and to prescribe treatment. These activities are however, geared towards identifying and supplying an *optimum environment* in which the body's natural healing mechanisms can operate freely. If I injure my arm in an accident, the doctor may x-ray the arm, he will clean the wound, he may set the bones, he may apply antiseptics, he may place a bandage and splint over the injury but he himself *will not do the actual healing.* The healing response lies within the individual and not with the doctor. Even from a religious stand-point, I feel it's questionable that a just God would elect to heal only those who could afford an air ticket to Lourdes. This healing mechanism comes hardwired into every human body.

Over the past eight years, I have reviewed hundreds of books, both popular and technical, and also countless research papers in the area of behavioural medicine and 'fighting back' and, with few exceptions, *virtually all* the people who achieved a miracle cure or spontaneous remission from cancer, heart disease or other significant condition, had also used the *very best of what modern medicine could offer.* To my knowledge, there is *no evidence* to support the use of 'alternative' therapies. What is offered here is intended as an adjunct to mainstream conventional medicine and not an alternative.

As a researcher, I have to look for the single factor, or group of factors, that is responsible for an observed outcome. As a psychotherapist or clinician working with human beings, I am allowed to speculate on inconclusive data and look for all possible applications, providing I follow the maxim "First, do no harm!" It is essential that theories in behavioural medicine be put to the test before being accepted into general usage. However, I also believe that if *anecdotal evidence* exists for a technique or approach, if it is certain that it *cannot harm* the patient, if it creates neither *'false hope'* nor *'false despair'*, if it is done with the knowledge of the patient's doctor, if it *does not put the patient at risk of exploitation*, then I am convinced that patients should have the option of making up their own minds.

I decided to write this manual because when I faced a health crisis of my own, there didn't seem to be a straightforward guide available on to *how* to fight back. This manual is a first edition and is *far from complete*. I doubt it will ever be complete, as new discoveries in the field of behavioural medicine emerge all the time. It is my ambition that it will be revised and updated on an annual basis, as new useful information come to light. Patients, carers and health professionals can also provide feedback for future editions, on their applications of what is contained here, and also on their own discoveries.

In expectation of future profits, multinational drug companies channel huge amounts of money into research. If one develops a successful protocol or programme in behavioural medicine, however, it immediately becomes available to all and is therefore not commercially attractive. This book is, and will continue to be, 'not for profit' in the hope of providing much need funding for research and training in behavioural medicine.

The 10 Principles of Fighting Back Effectively

(or how to create an Optimum Environment)

1. **Medical**: Get the best medical treatment available ASAP, and develop your medical team. Contrary to suggestions in the popular press, more than 95% of survivors followed their full medical regimen!
2. **Coach/Counsellor**: Get a coach/counsellor/ mentor and develop your support team to help you establish a well-formed outcome, to plan your plan and to work that plan.
3. **Exercise**: Develop an exercise plan consistent with your current physical and psychological condition and implement that plan starting very, very slowly and adding small increments weekly. This triggers the bodies own self-healing and pain control mechanisms
4. **Beliefs and Attitudes**: Review your beliefs and attitudes and the extent to which they may be affecting your illness and potential for recovery.
5. **Diet, Nutrition and Breath**: Explore your diet and nutrition and how you breathe.
6. **Use your mind** for change through self-hypnosis, meditation, affirmations, etc. Use these to reduce disease symptoms, manage side-effects of treatment and improve emotional well being.
7. Develop **life purpose** and **balance:** A bicycle that's going nowhere will fall over!
8. Get **social support** (clear out the 'weeds' and get new people (chosen this time!)
9. Look at **spirituality** in your life
10. Notice what's working and what's not working and **keep modifying your approach** until you get what you're after.

Why Fight Back?

Tipping the Scales is written for those people who want to make a difference. Research is now showing that patients who proactively participate in their own healthcare have a decided advantage. Frequently a patient, on diagnosis, will ask the doctor "What else can I do?". This book and future editions will seek to offer a possible response to that question, both for patients and their doctors. This is intended to be a survival, remission and recovery manual rolled into one, offering safe and 'evidence-based' approaches.

Some seriously ill people recover when others, with the same diagnosis, don't. As a therapist (and even as a patient myself) I tended NOT to ask myself: "Why are they so lucky?" I was much more interested in "How are they doing that?" If you are a patient, you might ask yourself which is the more useful question?

At a quantum level, Dr. Depak Chopra says that we humans replace all our soft tissue every ninety days, our skin every thirty days, a new liver every six weeks, a new mouth lining every three days, a new skeleton 98% every year. In other words, you are not the person you were even three months ago - your cells are constantly changing! Within the DNA of each cell, we carry a specific map or blueprint of perfection which the body constantly uses to rebuild itself. Even when someone has a tumour or a blocked artery, this too is changing, at a cellular level, every ninety days. We, as therapists and patients, need to discover how to restore the blueprint, and this is where psychosocial approaches are proving useful.

Its estimated we all produce at least 300 cancer cells daily, yet our immune system knows how to identify a cell that is not 'correct' and eliminate it. When we are depressed or ill, our immune function is often compromised, leaving space for opportunistic cancer cells to establish themselves.

Our job is to load the dice or *tip the scales* in the direction of optimum health, by providing *the very best possible environment* in terms of social interaction, food, emotional state and psychological well-being; also by changing damaging behaviours such as incorrect eating, smoking, excess alcohol consumption, addictions, short temper etc. We also need to deal with so-called 'negative' emotions, such as fear or confusion, which paralyse the individual and stops him or her taking steps to fight back. Greg Anderson of *Cancer Conquerors* says: "Retaining a medical team without doing all you can do to help yourself is like attempting to walk on one stilt".

Many doctors, in the course of their everyday practice, see patients engaging in unhealthy or dangerous behaviours. They try in vain to get their patients to eat more vegetables, drink less alcohol, stop smoking, eat less chocolate, take more exercise, practice stress-management etc. It is understandable why many physicians to-day have become disillusioned about persuading patients to change their lifestyles. We, as a society, have fallen into the habit of thinking that the doctor has a solution for everything and we, as patients, have to do nothing.

I believe that we are at risk of allowing the *lassitude* of healthy patients (not yet sick but engaging in unhealthy lifestyles) to blot out the enormous potential that discoveries in psychoneuroimmunology, or behavioural medicine, offers to patients. It is no longer disputed that what we eat, how we exercise, how we think and what we do, all combine to make us healthy or sick.

As a clinician, I find that, given the evidence that behavioural change will make a difference, clients and patients are willing to engage. Twelve years ago, Dr. Bernie Siegel, in his book *Love, Medicine & Miracles,* explained that less than twelve per cent of life-threatened patients were interested in fighting back. My experience in practice would suggest that, with the growing awareness among patients and their carers, this figure, today, is probably closer to twenty-five per cent.

Now the question is: should we offer behavioural programmes when people are life threatened? Are they more likely to take an interest in, or adhere to, a programme when they are looking down the barrel of a gun? As clinical research is now providing evidence that programmes can deliver statistically meaningful results, I believe:

1. Patients should be offered *education* regarding supportive behavioural programmes

2. Patients should be offered *choice* in these programmes

3. This choice should be offered *concurrent* with diagnosis

4. At a time when healthcare programmes are running out of money around the world and we are dealing with an increasingly ageing population, can healthcare

providers afford not to support such programmes? Professor Herbert Benson and Margaret Caudill at Harvard University demonstrated a fifteen per cent cost reduction by introducing such programmes. We, in Ireland, spend approximately £2 billion on health services.

When to Fight Back

Research suggests that you can produce meaningful clinical changes at virtually any stage in the progression of a disease. However, many patients wait until a disease has become well established before contemplating 'fighting back'. As we know that the immune system is our in-built 'fight back' or protection system, the following points are perhaps worth considering:

We know from clinical research that:

- *Bad news* lowers immune function
- Actual *diagnosis* (bad news) lowers immune function
- *Depression*, which often follows diagnosis, lowers immune function
- Medical *treatments* (chemotherapy, surgery, medication, radiation) lower immune function
- The sense of *powerlessness,* which often follows diagnosis, lowers immune function
- The sense of social *isolation*, common to many ill people, lowers immune function
- The disease may *stop physical exercise* (normally necessary for maintaining or enhancing immune function)
- The disease may interfere with *breathing* patterns - this can lower immune function

- The disease may cause *irregular sleep patterns* which can lower immune function

- The *progression* of a disease frequently lowers immune function

- *Feeling upset* often causes people to engage in ***damaging behaviours*** (such as increased alcohol consumption, smoking, overworking etc.) which lowers immune function

All the above happen *at the very time* when we need our immune function to be at its absolute strongest! Any medical programme which concentrates only on the disease and neglects consideration of and a specific strategy relating to the above is potentially deficient.

If your house was on fire, would you go out to lunch an leave it to the firemen? Why then, if your health is seriously compromised, would you leave total responsibility to the doctors?

Bubble Diagrams & Research

Throughout this manual you will find bubble charts, which emerged from the efforts of a behavioural medicine research group working with me since 1996. We were seeking to identify the significant potential **contributors to illness** and also the likely **contributors to wellness**; in other words, to distinguish the **essential** areas for **consideration** when a person is life-challenged?

The traditional approach has been to use the best of modern medicine plus **perhaps** one or two other complementary therapies and hope that this would do the job.

Human beings are complex and the genesis, or origins, of their diseases are equally so. What works for one person will not necessarily work for another. A particular drug may produce miracles in one person and do little or nothing for someone else.

Research in behavioural medicine to-day suggests that a structured synthesis of complementary approaches will produce a **synergistic** result. In other words, the interaction of a combination of different approaches produces an effect that **exceeds** the sum of their individual effects. This synergistic approach has been shown to be an effective adjunct to mainstream scientific medicine.

The absence of such a composite approach can result in a less than satisfactory outcome. A patient hearing about, say, meditation, may 'try' it for three or four weeks and then abandon it. However, clinical research on meditation will have indicated that it takes a **minimum** of eight to twelve weeks of sustained meditation before one might evaluate whether it was proving effective or not! Hopping from one thing to another can result in a life-challenged person **burning up** scarce time, money and energy (both physical and psychological) in 'trying' interventions.

Research is suggesting that it is necessary to come up with a specific **prescription** that matches the unique needs of the individual. As far back as the late 1970's, Dr. Hans Selye, the father of modern stress research and Dr. Richard Earle, the director of the Canadian Institute of Stress, noted that there was a major gap in the existing research on the relationship between stress, health and ageing.

Dr. Earle designed a research programme to investigate the relationships between these factors, by testing various existing stress-management techniques for their effectiveness in enhancing immune function and lowering body age.

Of the 1,868 who volunteered, 623 were selected who tested as having a body age significantly **higher** than their calendar age. Excluded from the programme were those in current medical treatment for any chronic physical disorder, or anyone in psychotherapy or on ongoing medication. After assessment, volunteers were trained in ten stress-management anti-ageing interventions:

1. Self-hypnosis and anti-ageing imagery
2. Nutrition
3. Values/goals clarification (career and leisure)
4. Relaxation
5. Physical conditioning (exercise)
6. Cognitive reappraisal (rethinking high-stress situations)
7. Personal goal setting and motivation
8. Communication and conflict resolution
9. Managing decisions, priorities and time.
10. Budgeting stress energy`

A **personalised** programme was designed for each individual which related specifically to their unique needs as revealed by psychological testing. Each participant undertook to follow this programme for eight months and to keep a daily diary of their experiences. The results achieved were nothing short of remarkable! After just eight months, they had achieved the following results:

- Average body age **decreased** by 8 years
- Doctor visits **decreased** by 53%*
- Days missed at work dropped by 58%*
- Below target blood pressure - 91%
- Weight within 10% of normal - 86%
- Cholesterol within target range - 74%
- Immunoglobulin A (IgA) **increase** - 31%*
- T cells **increase** - 28%*
- Triglycerides within target range - 61%

- Stress hyper-reactivity down - 46%*
- Stress recovery time **down** - 36%*
- Ability to relax at will **increase** - 31%*
- Physical strength increase - 39%*
- Body flexibility increase - 32%*
- Percentage body fat **decrease** - 36%*
- Oxygen uptake **increase** - 47%*
- Forced expiratory volume **increase** - 27%*

(Note: all figures are averages and asterisked items show the average improvement of the study group expressed as percentage changes from average baseline scores)

During this programme, the participants increased immune function by about 30 per cent (T cells and IgA). They enhanced their ability to take in and use oxygen by 35 per cent, indirectly increasing the efficiency of their lymphatic systems. They took eight years off their body age and all of these people were 'healthy'. Current research suggests that patients with cancer, heart disease and other significant health problems can produce **even greater** results.

What was unique about this research project was that, based on their specific behavioural and psychological profile, a personal **prescription** from the above interventions was prepared for each individual.

In much the same way, a patient engaging in a 'fight' back' programme (with limited physical and psychological resources), should be working with a programme which is well thought out and **relevant** to his or her needs, in order to make the best use of these resources,

Outside of strictly medical matters, more than **two hundred separate aspects** of the individual were identified as significantly impacting on a person's physical, psychological or spiritual well-being. These were deemed **worthy** of consideration before settling on any integrated recovery plan.

The bubble diagrams in this manual are intended as a brainstorming tool for the individual or for any health-care professional facilitating a person in fighting back. These are by no means the final word and we look forward to hearing from patients, their carers and professionals, with further ideas. Suggestions or feedback may be sent to the address at the front of this book.

Reference: Earle, R. & Imrie, D. (1989). *Your Vitality Factor.* London: Macmillan, ISBN 0-330-31704-0

Your Notes

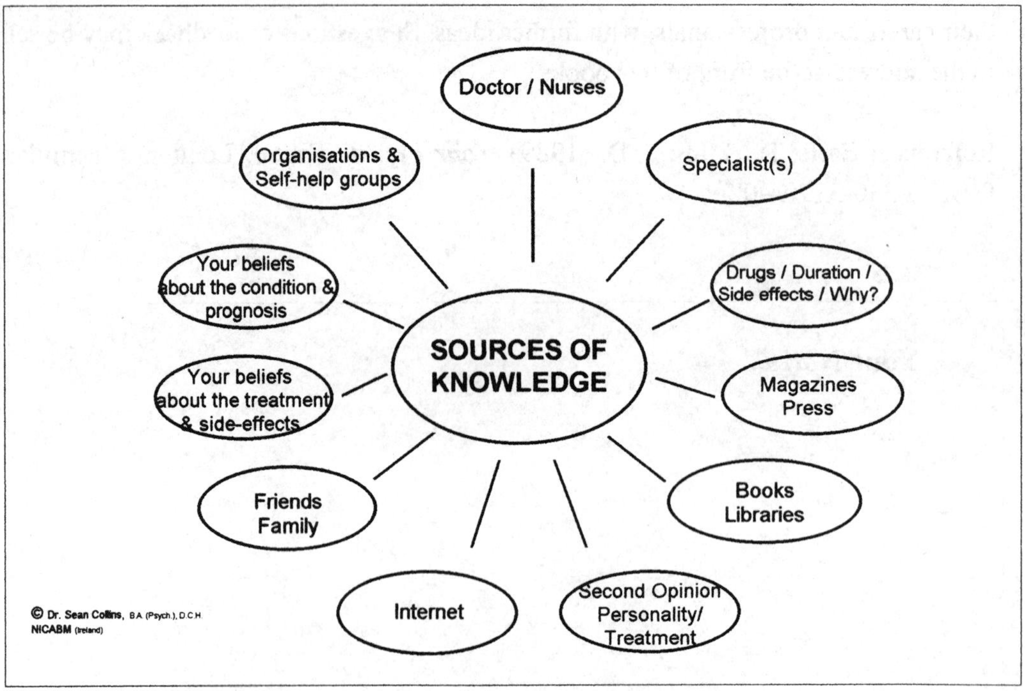

3. **Sources of Knowledge**: *Aspects of information/knowledge for consideration*

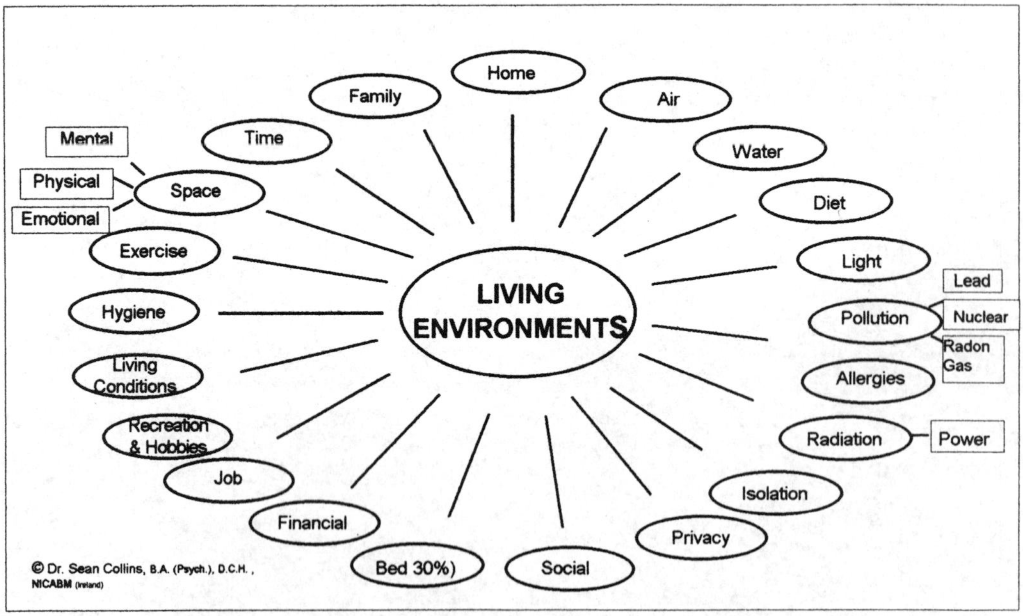

4. **Living Environment**: *The many environments within which we operate, which **significantly impact** on health and illness prospects*

Part 1

Background, Strategies and Considerations

Getting a Coach/Strategist/Health Crisis Counsellor

'Give sorrow words: the grief that does not speak,
Whispers in the overwrought heart and bids it break'
(Wm. Shakespeare)

If you are dealing with a major health problem, you are likely to be on an emotional roller-coaster, which can often leave a patient knowing what they *should* be doing in order to be healthier, but having trouble staying focused and on track.

Research suggests that having a clear-headed person fill the role of coach/strategist/ crisis counsellor, will result in far greater effectiveness in designing a 'fight back' plan, and a far greater *adherence* to that plan for recovery.

In an ideal world, the patient could call on a professional specifically trained for this role. In the real world, however, the task generally falls on untrained (but caring) shoulders. Here are some simple guidelines to assist the patient to identify a person or persons who might fill that role and to assist the carer in knowing how best to help.

Potential Mentors/Counsellors

- Profession health crisis counsellor (very few of them about!)
- GP or doctor (generally too busy)
- General counsellor/psychologist/psychotherapist
- Specialist councillor (for your disease/condition)
- Family member
- Friend
- Relative
- Work colleague

The Role of A Health Crisis Counsellor

Counselling refers to a helping process, the aim of which is *not* to change the person, but to help them access resources they already have for coping effectively.

Key Aspects in a Counselling Relationship

1. The sharing of concerns in a *confidential* environment.

2. Being in relationship with another person, which means *giving up* your own thoughts and interests for a while to be able to give your complete attention to the other person. It has been defined as "Taking responsibility for having someone else experience being understood by you".

3. Facilitating and encouraging the patient towards self-help.

4. Seeking to open up choices and options for the patient.

5. Seeking to understanding the problems of living with illness

6. Facilitating the patient to stay on track through regular review sessions

Features of a Helping Relationship

1. **Concreteness** - Accurately identifying and agreeing the problem and defining a well formed specific outcome.

2. **Time-scale** - Addressing, from the outset, the actual time required for implementing a programme for recovery, and to revise this as the process evolves (for patient and mentor).

3. **Confrontation** - Addressing essential and material issues honestly where appropriate. It does not infer aggressiveness. It means constructively pointing out discrepan-

cies between counsellor's and patient's viewpoints, or discrepancies between the patient's intentions, words and... what they actually do!

4. **Increased awareness** - Encouraging the patient towards increased self-understanding.

5. **Understanding/Empathy/Warmth** - Ensuring that the patient feels, without reservation, that they are understood, accepted and responded to genuinely by their counsellor/mentor.

6. **Expressiveness** - Encouraging the patient towards honest disclosure, and to be assertive and immediate in their reactions and responses.

7. **Open communication** - Openness from the counsellor and, when necessary, confronting, without playing the role of advisor or helper..

DON'Ts - in a Counselling Role

Don't:

Interrupt | Panic or look anxious | Interpret

Misinterpret | Take responsibility for change | Look out the window

Direct & lead more than is necessary | Judge and evaluate

Blame | Moralise, preach or patronise | Label or diagnose

Make judgements | Humour just to have the patient client feel good

Advise and/or teach (You 'should' or 'ought'...) | Interrogate

Over-interpret | Talk about yourself excessively or inappropriately

Automatically compare the patient's experience with your own

Try to put on a professional facade

Fake attention

Force the patient to be too brief

Have an answer for everything

Minimise or discount the client's feelings about what they see as a major trauma.

Don't invalidate the patient's feelings.

DO's in a Counselling Role

Do:

Help find out what problems there are

Help develop a well formed outcome

Challenge where appropriate

Communicate energy and commitment

Be an attentive listener

Remember to 'Shut up' sometimes

Be kind to yourself

Developing a Well Formed Outcome

The unconscious mind which effectively manages your body on a moment to moment basis is best guided or motivated by a precise, well-defined outcome or target. Patients confronting serious illness are often experiencing a degree of confusion in their thinking. The following brief model is used in areas such as medicine, business and counselling for developing such clear outcomes. Take the time to find as **many** possible answers to the following questions in order to enhance the clarity and effectiveness of your unconscious thinking.

1. What is your outcome? What do you *want* (rather than what you don't want!).

2. What are you *already* doing to achieve that outcome?

4. What stage are you at *now* in terms of achieving it?

5. What *will* you be doing to achieve that outcome?

6. What, specifically, will achieving that outcome *do* for YOU?

7. *Who* will benefit?

8. *How*, specifically, will they benefit?

   Is it just for *you*? For *others*? *Who*? Why for *them*?

9. How specifically will you *know* when you've achieved your outcome?

10. What *stops* you now or might stop you in the future?

11. What specific additional *resources* do you or might you need?

12. *When* do you need to have them in place?

13. What will you *gain* from achieving that outcome?

What *will happen* if you get it?

What *will not* happen if you get it?

What will happen if you *don't* get it?

What *will not* happen if you don't get it?

14. What, if anything, *will you lose* by achieving your outcome?

15. Is it *worthwhile*?

Reference: John McWhirter, Sensory Systems Training , Glasgow.

Your Notes

Secondary Gain

Secondary Gain could be loosely described as: a reason for holding on to your problem. Now, before you rise up in rage at the suggestion that someone would actually *want* to be ill, let me explain the concept further.

Our unconscious minds have a way of serving our needs by causing us to take on behaviour patterns that might, at a logical level, seem inappropriate or even ridiculous. For instance, someone wrestling for years with the problem of excess weight might, at an unconscious level, have several reasons for holding on to it. Without the weight, that person might be expected to engage in intimate relationships, play sports or go dancing; at one level the person wants these things, but there may be a deep-seated reason why the unconscious will not allow that individual to lose weight *until* the root cause has been addressed. A person with agoraphobia might appear to have a very restricted lifestyle; however, when they have let go of the fear, they also let go of a comfortable support system: the spouse won't have to come home early to keep them company and the children won't have to do the shopping!

Illness frequently has unconscious rewards; think back to a time (perhaps in childhood) when something vaguely unpleasant was looming - say, exams - and suddenly you developed 'flu' or earache. The symptoms were unpleasant, but the gain, both in parental attention and in avoiding the dreaded event, was worth the pain!

These symptoms are not fabricated; they are very real: a solution that is invented *outside of our conscious awareness.* So, the question to ask might be: 'If the problem or illness were to disappear, what do I lose?'

> Frequently, just the process of exploring the concept of *secondary gain* causes the problem to disappear.

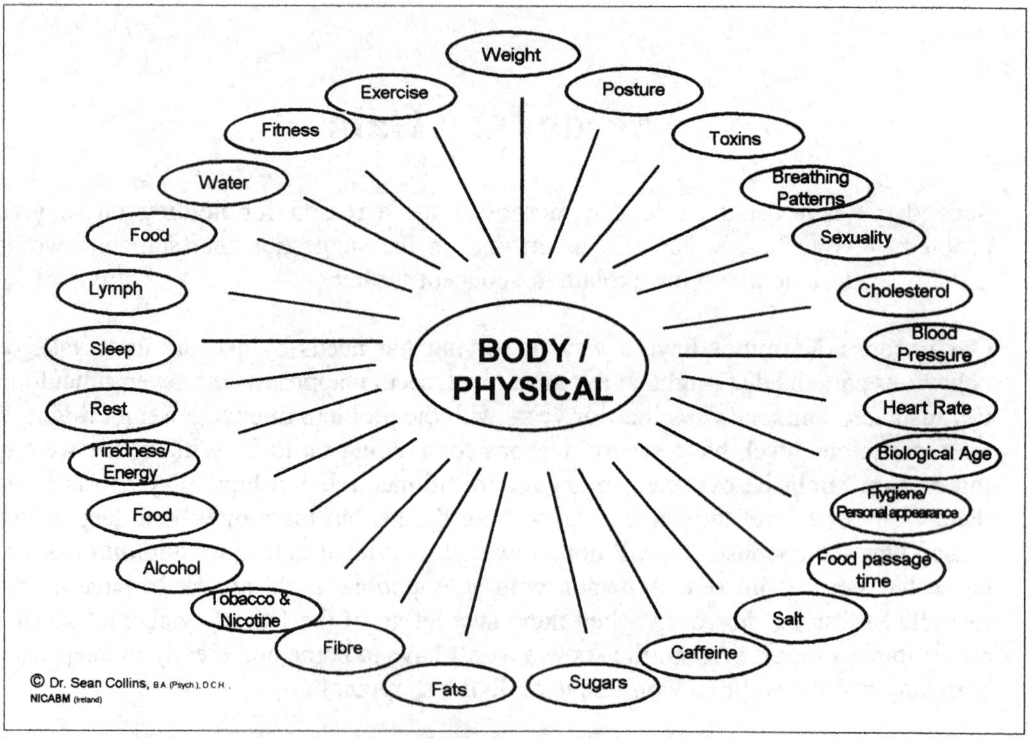

5. **Body/Physical**: *Factors affecting the body in its* ***ability*** *to fight back*

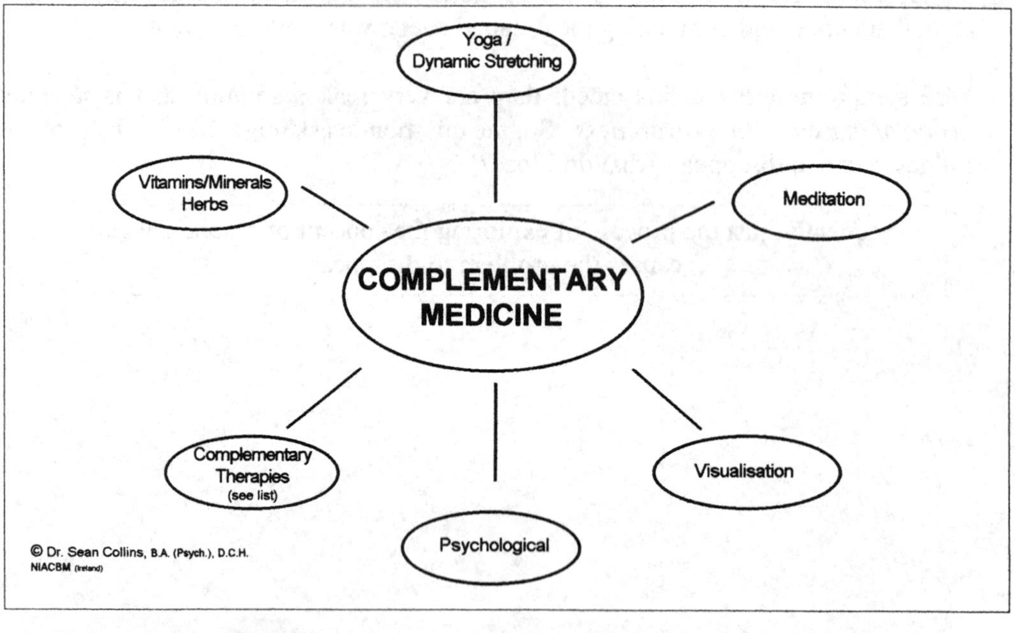

6. **Complementary Medicine**: *Elements of supportive or complementary medicine*

Priorities and Resource Management

Resources are mainly thought of as assets such as: money, possessions, attributes, skills, time, energy, confidence, family, friends, colleagues, and personal relationships. These components of life are often threatened when we are dealing with significant illness. Patients will frequently squander the most scarce of these resources, perhaps trying, at some unconscious level, to 'prove' that they are not sick.

Time

If you have been diagnosed with an illness, then the clock is ticking. Many people, when diagnosed, are frequently **quite healthy** physically, apart from some unexpected pain, a lump, or perhaps blood where there shouldn't be blood. In other words, they may be **98% well and only 2% ill.** Often the person's body, overall, is in excellent shape. However, we know that diagnosis can trigger a drop in immune function. We also know diagnosis can cause patients to adopt an 'illness' mind-set which makes matters worse. In no time at all, they are acting like 'ill' people.

Although it is virtually never too late, the best time to think about 'fighting back' in a structured fashion is **immediately** you have got your diagnosis or confirmation, when your body is in reasonably good shape and psychologically you're in good shape. You can start **that day**, creating an optimum environment in which your body's own 'fight-back' mechanism, the immune system, can function.

Energy

When we are ill, we are also often receiving powerful and toxic medical treatments and energy tends to be in short supply. As a therapist, I am appalled at how many clients don't want to be a nuisance to other people or don't want to disturb the 'status quo' by taking 'time out' for rest. Under normal circumstances, the body rebuilds itself when we sleep. When ill, we need even more rest and sleep. This is the time to be **absolutely uncompromising** in **prioritising yourself** and your body's need for rest; this is the time to 'nap' outrageously!

Confidence

Years ago I bought a book just for the title entitled '*You Can't Afford the Luxury of a Negative Thought, a book for people with any life threatening illness -- including life*" by John Roger and Peter McWilliams. When we are health-threatened, we need all the confidence we can get: confidence in ourselves, our bodies, our doctors, our medical treatment, our prognosis, our recovery capabilities.

Heralds of doom, 'helpful' friends who insist on telling you the worst, healthcare professionals who don't believe in your possibilities; these are all people to be ruthlessly purged from your life, at least if you're engaged in a 'fight-back' programme. Beliefs can heal and also can kill. What you read, what you watch on TV, who you spend time with, what you focus on have all been shown, in research, to impact on your immune system and your healing prospects.

Relationships

Social support and interaction have been shown to improve immune function and recovery prospects in illness, yet, the onset of illness places significant pressures on relationships at **the very time when they are most important**. Patients frequently retreat from relationships and activities, not wanting to be a 'nuisance'.

In implementing a 'fight-back' programme, it is essential to move towards positive supportive people and activities rather than away from them. Often, friends and family will tend to move *away* from ill people because they do not understand the illness, are frightened themselves or feel helpless, not knowing *how* to be of help. In a 'fight-back' situation, communicate to people how they can help with shopping, cleaning, finance, talking, etc. It is amazing how positive friends and relatives become when you make it clear how, *specifically,* they can help. **Positive** support groups have also been shown clinically to improve prognosis so, even if, at first, you don't like the idea of one, be self-ish and go looking for one now.

Money

I am constantly amazed at clients who will carry heavy bags of shopping to avoid spending £3 on a taxi fare even though, financially, they can well afford it. When you are life-threatened, you need to decide which is more important, energy or money, and nobody can decide that but you. However, it is essential that you at least consider and review how you allocate expenditure of money, as opposed to time, as part of your programme. You are seeking to offer an optimum environment to your body. Worries about money, which are not discussed with someone else, suppress immunity, so go and talk to someone if you have such worries.

Well-ness

When clients begin to engage in healthier eating, yoga, meditation and other similar approaches, they will often begin to feel better and have more energy, both physically and mentally. This is sometimes a risky period, in that they may then begin to take on more, to place more stresses upon themselves, and will squander the gains they have made and put themselves back at square one. When you begin to notice this feeling of 'well-ness' returning, as most people do, remember this is a time for caution!

Medical

Studies show that a majority of people (eighty to ninety per cent) with diseases, who engage in complementary or alternative approaches, do **not** tell their doctor what they are doing. This tends to be because they are afraid of having their hopes and ideas belittled or scoffed at. A frequent response form doctors tends to be " Well.....(long pause) ... it probably won't do you any harm" (Please note the unspoken presupposition "It probably won't do you any good either!").

In so far as is possible, work only with a doctor who is willing to respect **your** right to participate in **your own** healthcare (see notes on doctor/patient relationship). If your doctor or consultant does not respect this right, perhaps it is time to review your medical team.

To be successful in a fight-back programme, it is essential that you discuss with your doctor ***all*** complementary approaches you are using, **even** if he/she doesn't believe in them. You can request "If in your professional opinion, a specific complementary treatment doesn't represent a risk to me, and is unlikely to interfere in my medical treatment, then please keep your counsel and allow me to make my own judgement".

Your Notes

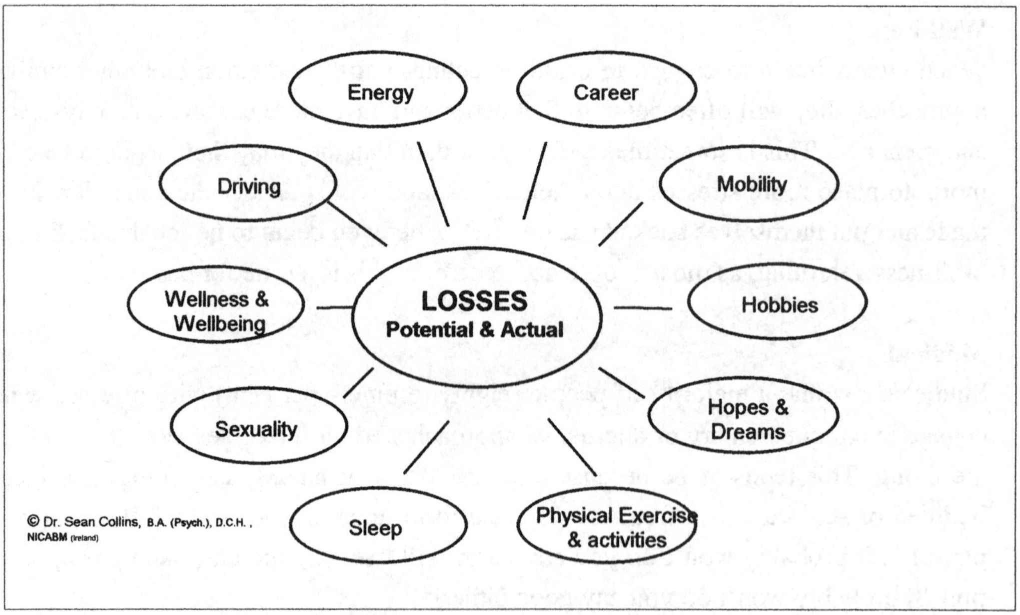

7. **Losses** (Potential & actual): *Losses patients experience. Noting them **and acknowledging them** aids healing!*

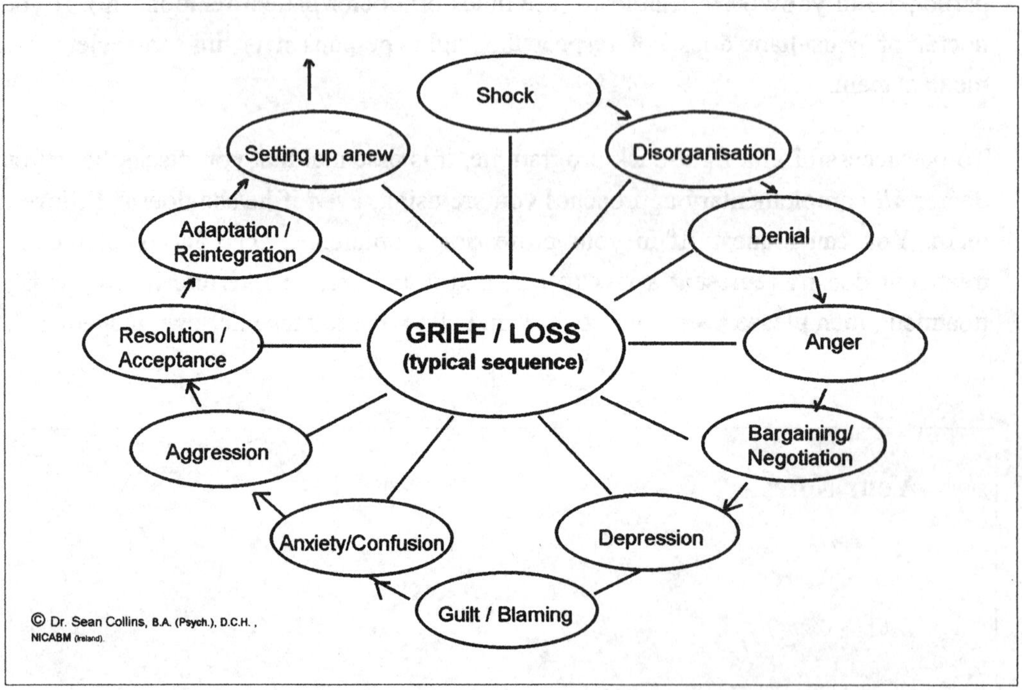

8. **Grief/Loss** (typical sequence): *Common stages in bereavement (remembering that human beings react in the way that is right for **them***

State Management and Anchoring

An anchor is any stimulus that produces a consistent emotional response pattern in a person. It can be either positive or negative. Cancer patients will sometimes report feeling nauseous at even the smell of the hospital or the sight of a particular medical person.

The following process can enable you to develop the ability to create a reliable triggering mechanism to elicit the emotional state you want, in any situation, without having to think about it! Your objective is the develop the ability to create a positive resourceful state, on demand, by a simple physical gesture such as joining the thumb and little finger of your left hand together and inhaling **sharply** through the nose.

Instructions:

1. Select one positive emotion from the following list and remember a time when you felt that emotion. Now identify what seemed like a peak moment in that situation.

2. As you recall it and the good feelings that went with it, mentally step back inside the memory for a moment, **as though you are there**, experiencing the good feelings (to the best extent that you can) and **as you experience them**, join the thumb and little finger of your left hand together and inhale sharply through your nose (so you can hear it) almost as though you are inhaling the good feelings. Immediately release the finger, the breath and the memory.

3. Now select another time when you felt really good (happy, confident, pleased, successful etc.) and again, identify the peak moment in that situation.

4. Repeat Step 2.

5. In each training session, associate the positive emotions of at least three good memories with the joining of the thumb and little finger and the rapid inhalation.

Four Keys to Anchoring: 1. Make sure you connect strong positive feelings to your resource anchor. Wishy-washy feelings will give you a wishy-washy anchor. 2. Timing - Join the thumb and little finger and inhale at the peak of the remembered good experience. 3. Make sure you apply the same pressure each time that you join the thumb and little finger.

Notes: Anchoring ensures always having access to your *greatest* resources! Much of human behaviour consists of unconscious pre-programmed responses - we are constantly anchoring; it's impossible not to! If anchors don't support or enable you, change or replace them with a new stimulus/response. Anchoring is neurological linking at the peak of an emotional response. The power or impact of an anchor is in direct ratio to the intensity of the emotion to which it is attached. For an anchor to be effective, when the stimulus is provided, the person must be in a fully associated congruent state (in the picture, seeing things through their own eyes), with the whole body involved! Anchors do not require lengthy conditioning. When a person is health-challenged, a positive anchoring method is essential for managing how you feel.

Do have *fun* in learning this process! After two to three weeks you can begin using this anchor to re-access your resourcefullness, when you feel challenged.

Your Notes

Please circle any of the following emotional states that YOU would definitely associate with being RESOURCEFUL (remember, there are no 'right' or 'correct' emotions). Then think back to some time in your life when you experienced that emotion. It is NOT necessary that you had an 'earth-shattering' time!

Think of a time you felt ....

A Winner	Adaptable	Appreciated
Bright	Brilliant	Calm
Capable	Caring	Cheerful
Clever	Committed	Compassionate
Confident	Connected	Content
Contributive	Creative	Curious
Decisive	Delighted	Determined
Dynamic	Energised	Enthusiastic
Excited	Fascinated	Flexible
Focussed	Forgiving	Free
Friendly	Generous	Grateful
Happy	Healthy	Hopeful/Optimistic
Imaginative	Control	Inspired
Integrated	Intelligent	Interested
Jolly	Joyful	Keen

Loved	Loving	Loyal
Magic	Organised/Structured	
Passionate	Peaceful	Powerful
Prosperous	Proud	Radiant
Relaxed	Resilient	Resourceful
Respected	Rich	Self Assured
Sharing	Spirited	Sprightly
Stimulated	Successful	Supportive
Unstoppable	Valued	Vital
Warm	Wonderful	Zestful
Carefree	Together	Other ___________
Other ___________		Other ___________
Other ___________		Other ___________
Other ___________		Other ___________

Your Notes

Depression

Depression is part and parcel of dealing with a life-threatening or 'quality of life' threatening illness. Patients will often try to deny that they are depressed or will perceive it as a sign of 'weakness' on their part to be hidden from the world. Depression has sometimes been described as a hiding place for us humans when things become too much to bear. Animals when they are sick retreat into quiet and dark places. We humans are not all that different.

However, if you are setting about fighting back, you can't afford the luxury of leaving depression unrecognised or untreated. This applies equally to patients and to their 'important others'. Such depression, if left untreated, tends to become worse and tends to monopolise much of your thinking time and energy.

There is no presupposition here that one 'ought' to get depressed if you are dealing with illness. Many people experience illness as a challenge and they rise to meet it. However, depression is sufficiently common and, potentially, is such a drain on your physical and emotional resources as to demand consideration in any 'fight-back' programme.

Symptoms of depression - a check-list

1. I regularly experience depressed moods and feelings
2. I get no pleasure from things I normally enjoy
3. I have difficulty concentrating
4. I have no interest in my normal hobbies or pastimes
5. I wake too early and can't get back to sleep
6. I find it hard to make decisions
7. I'm not performing efficiently at work
8. I have no inclination for sex or intimacy
9. My appetite is poor
10. I can't look forward to the future with any sense of pleasure
11. I get frequent headaches
12. I can't even enjoy watching television or doing a crossword

13. The mornings are worst
14. I'm tearful at times and have no control over this
15. I feel I can't cope
16. I feel guilty for having nothing I can justifiably complain about
17. The feeling that I ought to be able to 'get a grip' makes me feel worse
18. The thoughts of a holiday leave me cold
19. I've even thought of taking my life
20. I'm tired all the time

A diagnosis of depression should only be made by a trained health professional, doctor, psychologist, psychiatrist. However, if you can significantly identify with *more than two or three* of the above, then it's time to get some professional help. Dealing with a serious illness takes up a lot of time, and your time is precious - you cannot afford the luxury of wasting it. Seeking professional help will ensure that you have the physical and emotional energy to engage in a fight-back programme.

Your Notes

Presuppositions, Beliefs and Attitudes

Your pre-suppositions or beliefs about the world can determine whether you act effectively and create powerful results or whether you fail. They can be a block to action or, alternatively, they can provide interesting new ways of acting effectively and creating powerful results.

Beliefs are particularly important where serious illness is concerned. If a group of cancer patients are given an injection believing they are receiving chemotherapy, clinical trials have show that even though they are actually receiving only a water injection, approximately a third will experience hair loss. This mechanism in human beings is poorly understood but it demonstrates, clearly, the power of the mind to act. Presuppositions are not necessarily 'true'. They are simply a convenient or useful basis for ways of looking at, or interacting with, the world.

Review the following examples of 'presuppositions' and consider whether, if you were to adopt them (or at least some of them), how might they impact on the progression, regression or cure of your illness?

1. The meaning of your communication with other people is the response you get. This may and often will be different from what you intended! (Communication often breaks down in the face of serious illness.)

2. People have all the ability they need to succeed; there are no unresourceful people, only unresourceful states of mind! If even one person can do something - heal themselves or experience remission - then potentially, within reason, you can do it too!

3. You, and only you, are in charge of your mind and therefore the results. Professionals may predict your future but only **you** can determine it.

4. If you always do what you've always done, you'll always get what you always got! If you want something different, then do something different. Survivors almost always radically change some aspects of their lives.

6. There is no such thing as 'failure', there is only feedback. 'Failure' offers a unique opportunity to learn something you might otherwise have missed. In other words, keep going.

7. Success is the result of good judgement. Good judgement is the result of experience. Experience is often the result of bad judgement.

8. Beliefs are only beliefs and not facts. All beliefs can be challenged.

Reference: Anthony Robbins, Awaken the Giant Within. (6)

Your Notes

The Immune Power Personality

Current research suggests there are specific personality traits that are *helpful* in stimulating immune function and other traits which are *unhelpful* (please note I did *not* say 'good' or 'bad'). The research suggests that positive traits are potentialities in all of us, and **can be awakened** through awareness, short term therapy or practice.

In case anyone thinks of feeling guilty about their personality traits, may I suggest that nobody in their right mind sets out to create a disease or illness for themselves. We don't receive an owner's manual when we're born and, as children, we don't have the gift of foresight. It's not surprising that we inadvertently develop 'unhelpful' personality traits. As we, as infants, begin to adapt to the world around us we noticed that crying brought food and comfort, and later on we used that behaviour to get parental attention. At the toddler stage we discovered which behaviour brought us smiles and rewards and which brought punishment. Little girls were encouraged to be kind, caring, meek and obedient; little boys were rewarded for being brave, tough and competitive.

Strange as it may seem, these personality traits which we developed to help us survive the trials of childhood are often those which, if taken to extreme in adult life, can predispose us to serious illness. Acknowledging possession of these traits, can now enable you to review and change them (ideally with the help of a training course or professional counsellor/therapist).

The following concepts are the result of extensive scientific studies. With the exceptions of Alan Luks (whose work has been validated elsewhere), all are psychologists or psychiatrists of note who have conducted original studies published in leading scientific journals.

These concepts are distinct but overlapping.........

1. **Attend, Connect & Express** - People who actually notice or attend to their own mind-body signals of discomfort, pain, fatigue, distress, sadness, anger, and pleasure cope better and have better immune profiles, and a healthier cardiovascular system according to Psychologist, Gary Schwartz, Ph.D., of University of Arizona.

2. **Capacity to Confide** - James Pennebaker, Ph.D., has demonstrated that individuals who confide their secrets, traumas and feelings to themselves **and** others have livelier immune response, healthier psychological profiles, faster recovery from illness and far fewer incidences of illness (see technique for journalling).

3. **Hardiness, Commitment, Control & Challenge** - Susanne Ouellette, Ph.D., a psychologist at the City University of New York, originated the concept of personality *hardiness.* This quality which cause people to experience fewer chronic illnesses and symptoms and have stronger immune systems comes from the "three Cs": a sense of *control* over one's quality of life, health and social conditions; a strong *commitment* to one's work, creative activities, or relationships; and a view of stress or disease as a *challenge* rather than a threat.

4. **Assertiveness** - George F. Solomon, M.D., an early pioneer in PNI, conducted some of the earliest studies on personality and immunity. He showed that people who assert their needs and feelings have stronger, more balanced immune responses. They more readily resist and overcome a range of diseases associated with dysfunctional immunity - from rheumatoid arthritis to AIDS.

5. **Affiliative Trust** - David McLelland, Ph.D., a world renowned psychologist of Boston University, has discovered that individuals who are strongly motivated to form relationships with others based on unconditional love and trust, rather than frustrated power, have more vigorous immune systems and reduced incidence of illness.

6. **Healthy Helping - Altruism** - Health Investigator, Alan Luks, conducted a large survey showing that people committed to helping others, displaying the personality trait of altruism, suffer far fewer illnesses and recover faster.

7. **Self-Complexity** - Patricia Linville, a psychologist at Duke University, has demonstrated that people who explore many facets of their personality, called 'self-aspects' (or explore what it means to be human), can better

withstand stressful life circumstances. These people are less prone to stress, depression, physical symptoms and infections in the wake of such stressful life events.

Characteristics of the Miracle Prone

(Those who get sick *and recover*!!)

The following are common characteristics identified in over 2,500 so called 'miracle' cases reported in medical journals.

To have an *open mind*, want to be cured, but *not* to approach fighting back with this as the single-minded purpose of their journey.

To be in a state of psychological void, with an *openness* to paradox, mystery, and the fullness of life.

To have made or be making a shift from dependency to *autonomy*. Noticing a subtle change in belief system from feeling 'out of control' to feeling that the process of healing comes from within rather than without.

To have made spiritual changes involving connection of mind, body & spirit.

To have a confidence and awareness beyond the rational, logical, simplistic knowledge of everyday life

To possess a *yearning for much more from life* than mere coping, survival, success and security. To transcend the here and now, actively searching for the meaning of life (see life planning).

To have a tendency to be a psychic gambler, a willingness to take risks for the fulfilment of dreams, and a predilection to think in a freewheeling style that reflects the uncertainty of life.To be flexible and adaptable, emotionally biphasic and paradoxical with strong mood fluctuations. That is to **express** feelings and to be as passionate about grief as about joy. Being expressive about the disease is a key aspect.

"They're not one way or the other being. They are *both* one way *and* the other -logical and intuitive, confident and self-critical, co-operative and rebellious, spiritual and irreverent, consistent and unpredictable, hopeful and despairing".

They are complex and paradoxical. They acknowledge the contradictory parts of themselves, are comfortable with who they are and find their own songs to sing rather than imitating the songs of others who have been healed. There's no point in using the neighbour's key to open your door! It is a *key* but it's unique!

The biggest barrier to developing a 'survivor' personality comes from having been raised a 'nice' person.

(Grateful thanks to O'Regan, Hirshberg, Siebert and Pearsall)

Your Notes

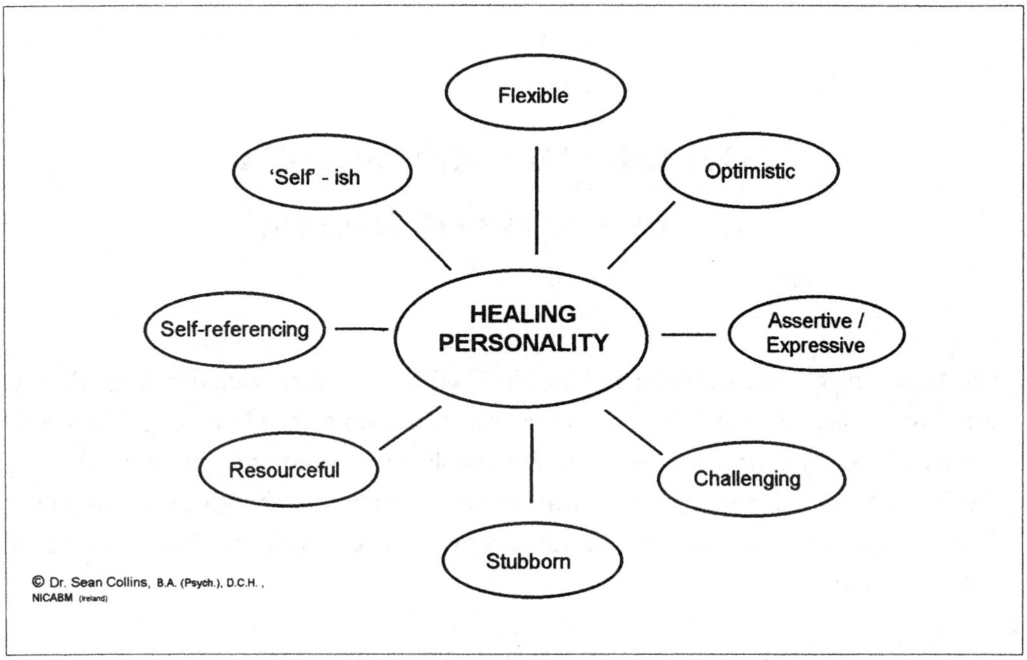

9. **Healing Personality**: *Personality traits identified with remission, healing and the* ***'miracle prone'***. *These can be built upon or enhanced!*

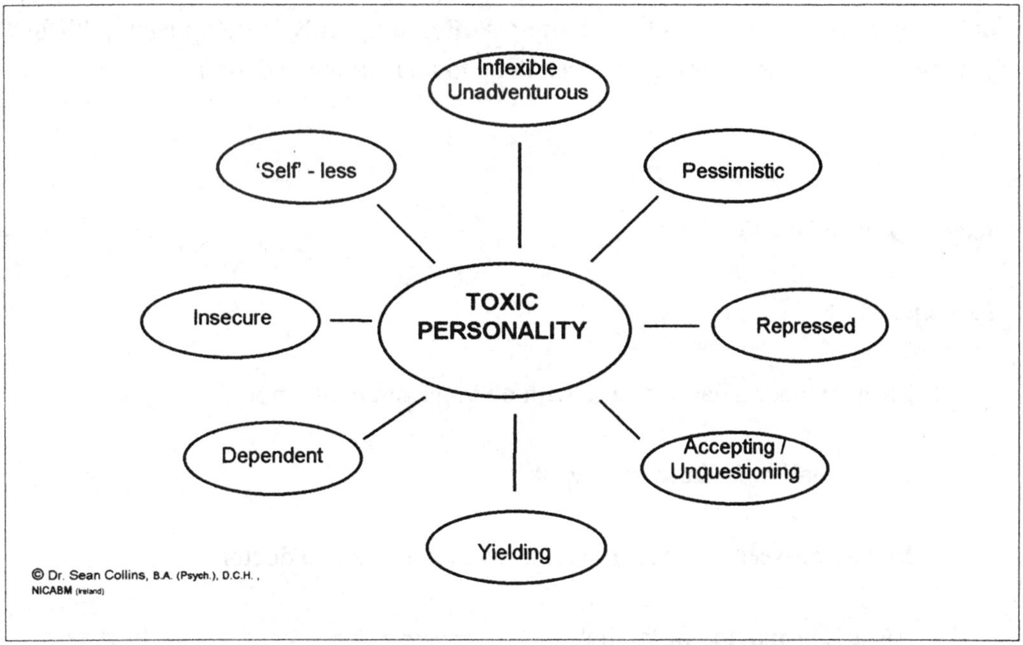

10. **Toxic Personality**: *Personality traits NOT identified with remission, healing and the* ***'miracle-prone'***. *These can be modified or changed!*

Winning the fight against Coronary Heart Disease

Until recently, doctors believed that the No. 1 killer in western societies, heart disease, was irreversible. In 1990 the prestigious medical journal, the Lancet, published the results of a study carried out by Dr Dean Ornish, M.D., who at the time was head of the Preventive Medicine Research Institute, and a faculty member of the University of California, at San Francisco. His research showed conclusively that this belief was no longer tenable.

In his study, Dr. Ornish demonstrated that heart victims could clean out their arteries provided they had the grit to make radical changes in their lives. One participant said "the programme requires a heavy dose of dedication". Miracles are performed every day in by-pass operations, but these arteries often frequently close up again; "Why?" you may ask; because nothing has been done to address the underlying causes.

Key Aspects of the Ornish Study

Participants -

1. Spent an hour a day working with on yoga and meditation

2. Took a half hour daily brisk walk

3. Met twice weekly in group with a psychologist and a doctor

4. Ate a 15% maximum fat diet

Results of the Ornish Study

- 82% of the participants experienced significant improvement
- The more a patient engaged with the programme, the more effect he produced (known as a 'dose' effect)
- The average degree of blockage reduced from 61% to 56% (a 17% increase in oxygenated blood flow to the heart muscle)
- Some completely blocked arteries actually opened
- 91% reported a drop in heart pain, generally within weeks of starting
- Angina disappeared in many cases
- Cholesterol, in many cases, was cut in half
- HDL, the 'good' cholesterol increased
- Severe blockages are the most likely to regress
- Participants said that if they had not had the group support, they could not have kept going in going for a total lifestyle change

Dr Dean Ornish's programme for Reversing Heart Disease, Random Century, 1990 ISBN 0-7126-4896-8 (hb) or 0-7126-5011-3 (pb)

This is essential reading for anyone who has heart disease

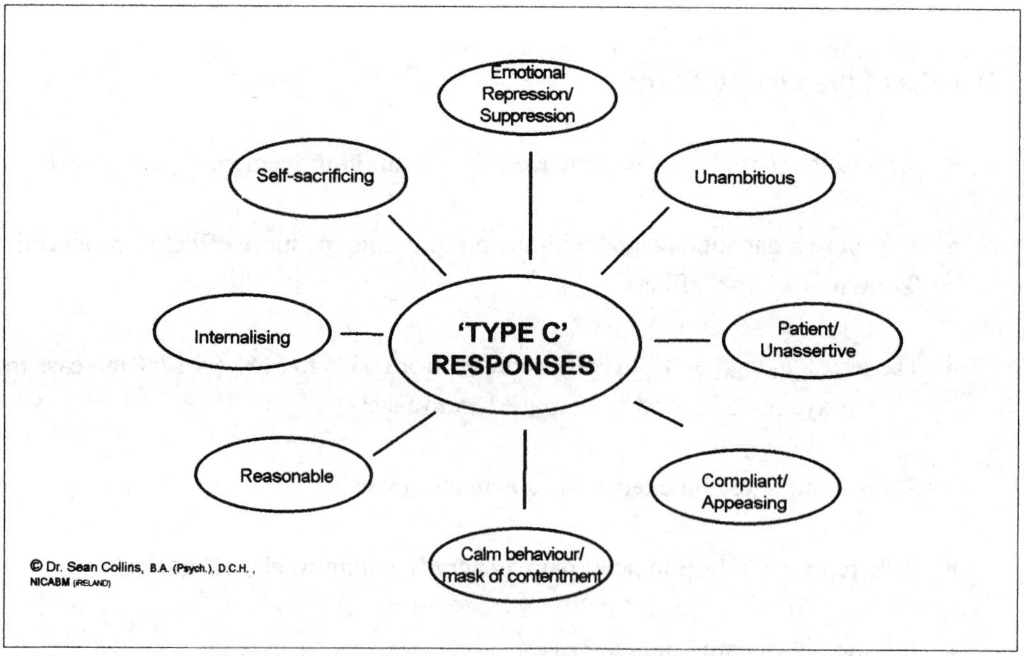

11. **'Type C' Responses**: *Personality traits frequently identified with* ***cancer****. These can be modified or changed!*

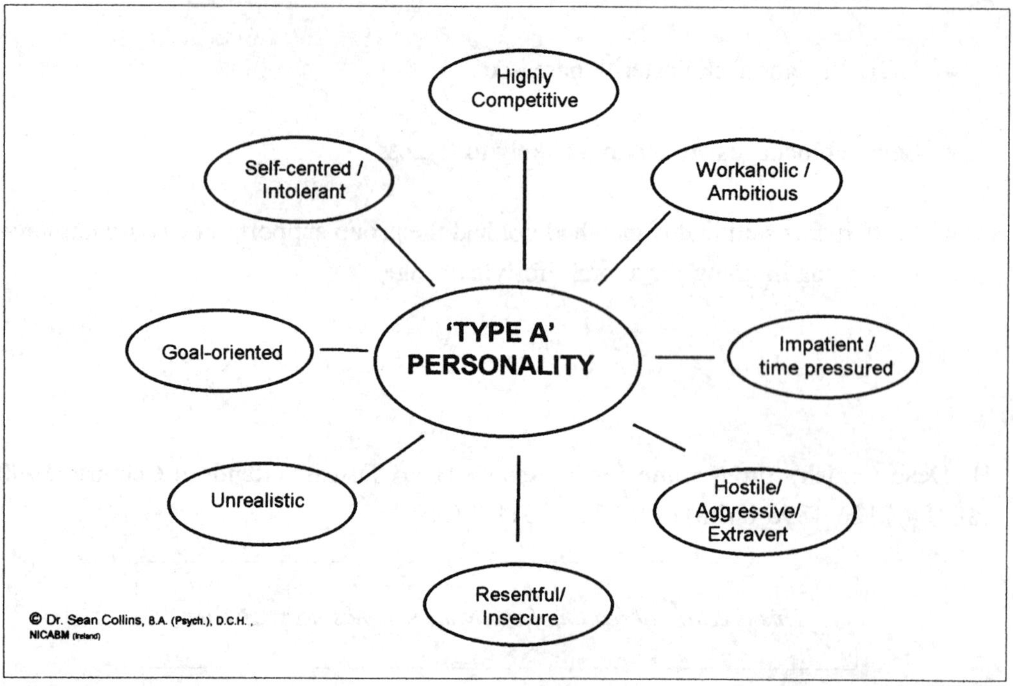

12: **'Type A' Personality**: *Personality traits frequently identified with* ***heart disease***

Cancer - Ground Breaking Discovery

Professor David Spiegel is a professor of Psychiatry and Behavioural Sciences at Stanford University School of Medicine, one of the leading Universities in the world. He is on the editorial boards of eleven medical journals and his research work has been widely published.

In the late 80's he set out to prove that behavioural or psychosocial interventions could **not** affect the occurrence or progression of cancer. Whilst there were claims being made by people like Dr. Bernie Siegel, Dr. Carl Simonton and others, there was little hard evidence to show that patients could make a difference in the progression of their illness.

Professor Spiegel used a study of 86 women with very advanced (Stage 4) metastatic breast cancer. To his surprise, rather than proving that psychological intervention was useless, he found that there had been a doubling of average life expectancy between the intervention group and the control group, and that some of the women from the intervention group were still alive 13 years later!

This study has been subjected to rigorous methodological challenges and was published in *The Lancet*: October 14th, 1989, and in other major medical journals around the world.

His approach, called 'supportive-expressive group psychotherapy' included exploration of forming strong bonds of mutual support, facing fears of dying and death directly, re-ordering of life priorities, managing relationships with family, friends and physicians, and learning to control pain and other symptoms and side-effects of treatment using self-hypnosis.

A similar well-documented study, carried out by Fawzy I. Fawzy, a researcher at UCLA Medical School, showed that participants had better immune function, lower rate of tumour recurrence and a dramatically lower death rate.

Whilst these studies, and others like them, are not the final word on the matter, they provide compelling evidence for using such adjunctive approaches.

Details of his research and program are in *Living Beyond Limits* by David Spiegel, MD published 1993 Random House Books ISBN 0-09-178641-X

Your Notes

Deep, Dark Secrets

"Am I he who would give to the world
the love I cannot give to myself?"

Words found scribbled in the diary of a heart attack victim dated three weeks before his death.

Human beings often have aspects of themselves which they like to keep private or secret. Time and again, we read in the media of public figures, church leaders, professionals emerging as being very 'human'. The sorts of secrets that come out include theft, dishonesty, cheating, betrayal of trust, inadequacy, business failures, academic failures, illicit affairs/relationships, sexual issues (masturbation, cross dressing, perversions, fetishes etc.), resentments, homosexuality (although now more widely accepted, many gay people feel forced to remain in the 'closet'), hatreds, jealousies, fears, phobias (social contact, public speaking, animals, travel etc), alcoholism, drug abuse, eating disorders (bulimia and binge eating), mental illness and so on. The list is endless.

However, current research is now demonstrating that the suppression of 'deep dark secrets' can accelerate the progression of various illnesses. Conversely, similar research is showing that talking about or even writing about these 'secrets' can enhance our immune function and help move us towards wellness. So, if you are seeking to 'tip the scales', then it is well worth while considering any such events from the past and 'flushing them out' with something like the Pennebaker process, or with a trained counsellor or psychotherapist. It is useful to bear in mind, as you think this through, that as we grow from childhood to adulthood, events are stored away in the unconscious *through the eyes of, or from the perspective of a child.* And the feelings we have attached to these events will be the child-like feelings we had back then. Even though we may have long since thought an event was resolved, those powerful emotions may still be there, blocking our recovery.

Challenging Limiting Beliefs

Your beliefs determine your response or sense of power in relation to everyday events. As a patient, some of these beliefs will be empowering, such as: "I have a powerful healing body" and some may be negative or disempowering, such as: "I'm never going to get well".

Negative beliefs can deny a person access to their own capabilities. If an asthmatic, allergic to flowers, is exposed to a very realistic but artificial rose, they will most likely experience a asthma attack based purely upon their belief that it is real. In countries like Haiti, if the witch doctor points the bone at someone, or places a curse on them, they will probably die! This phenomenon has been studied by scientists for many years and is still little understood. The converse also applies. There have been cases where patients with cancer were inadvertently told, due to a mix-up in X rays, that their cancer was gone. When the mix-up was subsequently discovered and the people were checked, in some cases, the cancer had disappeared completely!

A famous case from the annals of medical history was a certain Mr. Wright, who was suffering with terminal cancer and had only weeks to live. He talked his way onto a test panel for a new anti-cancer drug called Krebiozen. Within a week of receiving the drug, his cancer specialist described Mr Wright's tumours as shrinking "like snowballs in a hot oven" and he went into complete remission. Some months later, doubts were expressed in the media about the efficacy of Krebiozen. Mr Wright's tumours returned almost immediately. His oncologist, who had been amazed at the original disappearance, now engaged in a deception (which would ethically not be acceptable to-day). He informed Mr. Wright that the original batch of Krebiozen had been 'defective' in some way, and would Mr. Wright like to receive the new 'Super Enhanced Krebiozen. Mr Wright enthusiastically agreed.

There was no 'Super' Krebiozen and what the doctor actually injected was sterile water. Mr. Wright's tumours again disappeared "like snowballs in a hot oven" and he returned to his normal life. Three months later, an announcement was made in the medical media that Krebiozen was judged to be worthless. Mr Wright learned of this, his tumours returned almost immediately, and he died shortly afterwards.

Henry Ford once said "Whether you believe you can, or whether you believe you can't, you're right!". Most beliefs are simple generalisations from the past, based on our interpretations of both painful and pleasurable experiences. They do however have a significant impact on our abilities to think, to do things, and most importantly, to motivate ourselves. Beliefs are, however, nothing more than a feeling of **certainty** about something.

In the context of healing, beliefs are neither 'right' nor 'wrong'. What is worthy of consideration is: are they useful? If a person believes himself have an incurable disease, what is the likelihood of a cure?

How to challenge unuseful beliefs

Step 1: Make a list of any negative or 'disempowering' beliefs which you currently hold about: yourself, your body, your health, your prognosis and perhaps about your belief in your ability to motivate yourself to do whatever needs to be done to create or achieve an optimum healing opportunity?

Step 2 : Make a list of your 'empowering' beliefs about yourself, your body, your healing capability and your ability to motivate yourself.

> Note : Most beliefs were useful at one time or in some particular context. However, this usefulness can, and often does, change with the passage of time.

Step 3: Now begin to challenge the 'limiting' or 'disempowering' ones, one at a time.

1. How is this belief ***ridiculous*** or absurd?

2. Where, or from whom, did I get this belief? Is there an alternative?

3. Was this a ***worthwhile*** source?

4. What will it ultimately cost me emotionally if I don't ***let go of this belief***?

5. What will it ultimately cost me health-wise if I don't ***let go of this belief***?

6. What will it ultimately cost me in relationships if I don't ***let go of this belief***?

7. How specifically will my life change for the better when I have dumped this belief?

8. What beliefs would be more useful? Who currently has these? What can I do to acquire such beliefs?

9. What is the longest time a person has survived (with quality of life) with this condition/disease? What did they do?

Note: Consider ***repeating*** this challenge daily for four to five days.

Your Notes

Challenging Negative Self-Talk

Its not what happens to you in life that is important. Rather, it's the *way you respond* to those events that counts. The *habitual* questions you ask yourself such as "why does this always happen to me?" or "why are other people so lucky?" determine the way you interpret and evaluate your experiences and ultimately the quality of your life.

When serious illness strikes, our internal conversation become even more important. What we focus on tends to expand. Depression, which has a negative effect on the immune system, is frequently triggered by our internal conversations with ourselves and what we focus on.

Researchers and writers, such as Dr. Tom Rusk, Anthony Robbins and Steve Andreas, Ph.D. (see reading list), encourage asking yourself 'different' questions from those you habitually ask so as to shift your 'habitual' orientation!

Seven Day Challenge

For a period of seven days, explore starting each morning by asking yourself the following specific questions and really commit to exploring the answers that emerge. Of course it's easier to ask yourself the other 'awfulising' questions... but, is it *useful*?

In my life right now..........

1. What am I **happy** about?

2. What could I be happy about?

3. What am **excited** about?

4. What could I be excited about?

5. What am I **proud** of?

6. What could I be proud of?

7. What am I **grateful** for?

8. What else could I be grateful for?

9. What do I **really enjoy** in life?

10. What am I **committed to**?

11. What could I be committed to?

12. Who do I **love** and who loves me?

13. What could I actively do to-day to improve any/all of those relationships?

14. With any event/occurrence that went 'poorly' yesterday, what did I learn, or could I have learned, from that experience, the **learning** of which would now **allow** me to **let go** of any negative feelings and feel happier?

Your Notes

Sleep

When a human body is challenged by illness, compounded by the side-effects of medical treatment, it requires **more rest and recovery** time. This is also often a time when people experience broken sleep patterns. As a therapist, I am frequently appalled at clients who mistakenly believe that taking sleeping tablets would be some sort of admission of 'failure', or that taking a nap is in some way indicative of 'giving in' to the disease. The reality is that even a healthy body needs six to eight hours a day to repair and rebuild itself. If it is denied this, it becomes ill very quickly. It is, therefore, just common sense to offer a challenged body **even more time** to assist in healing itself.

A common characteristic identified among 'survivors' is their ability to be **'self-ish'** and to take additional time for sleeping. They do not wait for the body to become debilitated or exhausted. They adopt a napping process early! Researchers often comment on the lower incidence of heart disease and cancer among the Mediterranean populations and frequently attribute this to diet. Some recent finding suggest that part of the effect may come from the habit of taking a 'siesta' in midday. Even a 20-30 minute doze or snooze has been shown to be effective in allowing the body to restore its batteries. Here, the animal kingdom also provides a lesson. When animals are sick, they sleep.

Sleep Thoughts

1. You need **more sleep** when you are health-challenged.

2. If your sleep is broken, **get help** in the form of medication, hypnosis or self-hypnosis.

3. **Naps** are invaluable, and can be taken anywhere. All you have to do is become sensitive to the needs of your body.

4. The time to start napping and getting more rest is **when you are first diagnosed**, not when you are exhausted and run down.

5. Adopting a different sleeping strategy and addressing sleeping difficulties promptly during recovery is simply putting your shoulder behind your own self-healing mechanism.

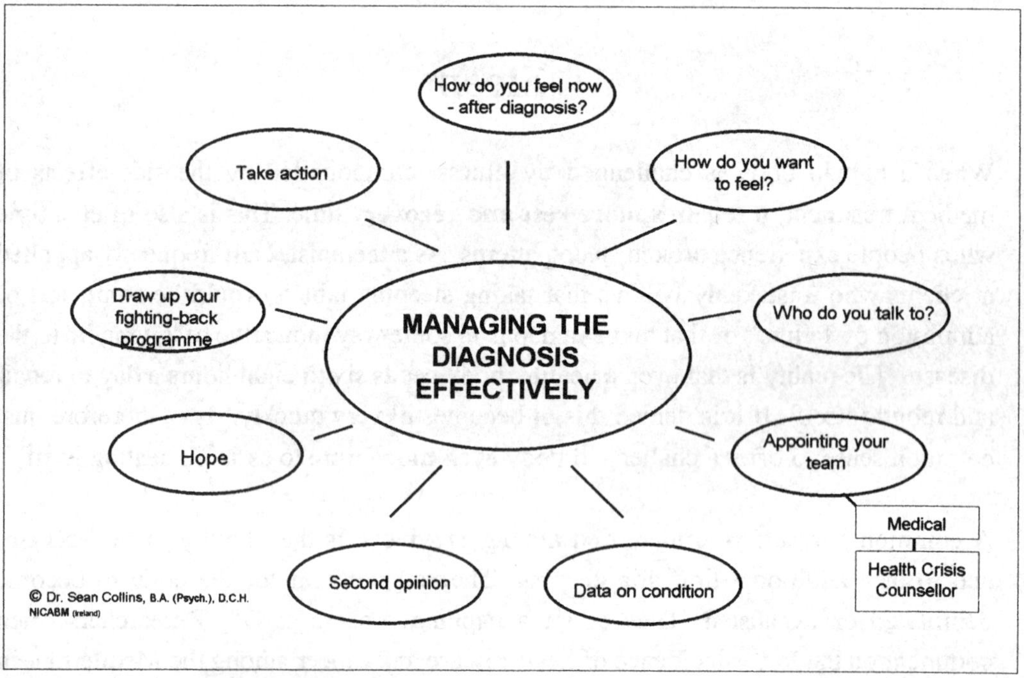

13. **Managing the diagnosis effectively**: *Aspects of the diagnosis for* ***essential*** *review*

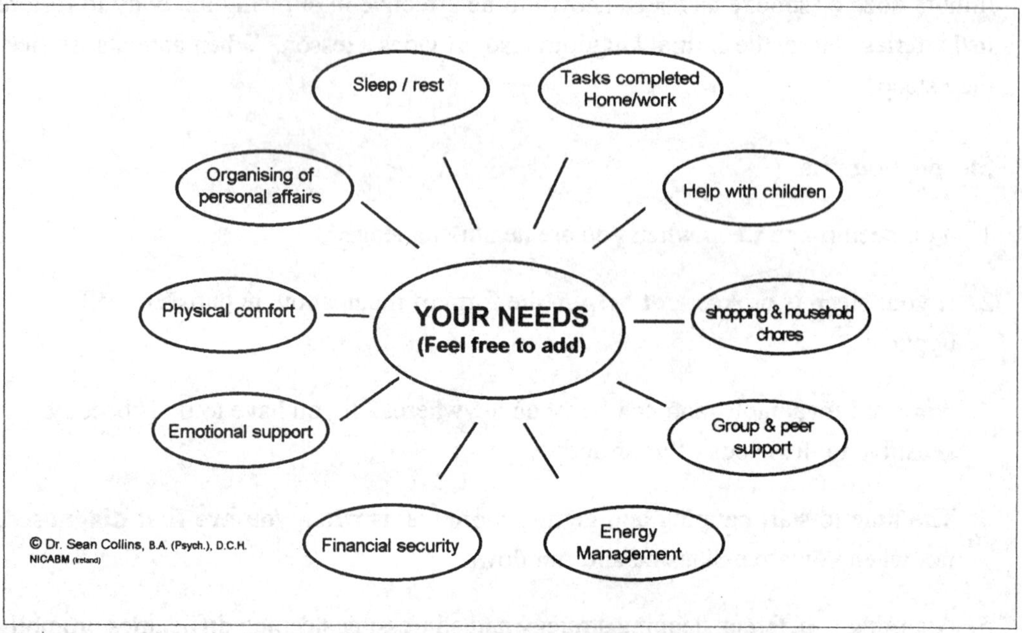

14. **Your needs**: *Looking after No.1! Essential considerations for* ***immediate*** *review*

Stress Management & Relaxation Training

"My crown is in my heart, not on my head;
Not decked with diamonds and Indian stones, nor to be seen;
My crown is called content;
A crown it is that seldom kings enjoy."

- William Shakespeare, Henry VI, part III

Stress

Scientists are now beginning to show that up to 90% of man's diseases are psychosomatic or stress related. Our automatic stress-response causes the pulse rate to shoot up, blood pressure soars, the stomach and intestines stop all the busy activity of digestion, hearing and smell become more acute. Hundreds of other physical changes occur without our even knowing it. With stress comes a sharp increase in energy consumption. The reaction puts the entire body in a state of readiness, and whether the cause of the stress is inside the body or out, it will often cause a person to be completely drained.

Does this sound like how you want to feel when you need to trigger a healing response? Probably not! Serious illness, unfortunately, can cause enormous, and frequently ongoing, stresses to the body. My objective here is to encourage you to consider what stress is, what causes it, and how you can best manage it so as to enhance your healing response.

The chemistry of stress

Any form of stress, whether from overwork, quarrelling, redundancy or illness, will cause electrical and chemical messages to be carried along nerve pathways to a part of the brain called the hypothalamus. This part of the brain controls much of the rest of the nervous system, both within the brain itself and outside, and in all parts of the body. It produces a chemical known as the corticotrophin releasing factor, known as CRF, which is sent down one of the two pathways. The first pathway is the pituitary gland, in the middle of the brain, which is stimulated to produce another chemical messenger called adreno-corticotrophic hormone, or ACTH. This enters the bloodstream and travels on to the cortex, or outer part of the adrenal glands, which are situated directly on top of the kidneys. The adrenals are thus stimulated to produce cortisol, a chemical that increases blood sugar and speeds up the body's metabolism.

On the second pathway, messengers leave the hypothalamus and trigger electro-chemical impulses down the brain stem and spinal cord until the signals reach the core of the adrenal glands. The result is a release of adrenalin (epinephrine), which helps supply extra glucose to serve as fuel for the muscles and brain and noradrenalin, which speeds up the heartbeat and raises blood pressure. Both tracks feed back to the pituitary to regulate further the stress responses.

Dr Hans Selye, the father of modern stress research mapped the hormonal pathways almost 50 years ago. Since then, scientists have found that stress provokes a number of even subtler chemical changes in the body that may have profound effects on health, both physical and mental. "There is a constant intertwining of stress systems." says Stanford neurochemist, Jack Barchas, "It's much like a symphony". Over the past two decades, researchers have learned that stress triggers chemical changes in the brain. Particularly sensitive to emotional strains are the concentration of potent chemicals, called neurotransmitters, which act as messengers between nerve cells.

Among these messengers are serotonin, adrenalin, noradrenalin (norepinephrine), acetylcholine and dopamine. In a study at Stanford University, rats were forced to swim in water at four degrees centigrade, for three minutes. Examination of their brain tissue afterward revealed that levels of noradrenalin had fallen by twenty per cent, and adrenalin by thirty to forty per cent. Scientists also discovered that the body produces its own pain-killers, morphine-like chemicals called endorphins. Stress boosts the production of these analgesics and raises our pain threshold. This may explain the mystery of why seriously injured soldiers often feel no pain, or why footballers sometimes play with fractured bones, not feeling any pain until after the match.

Because it alters the body's chemical balance, more and more research points to stress at least increasing the probability of serious illness, if not, in fact, being a *cause* in itself. Depression has also been associated with low levels of two neurotransmitters: serotonin and noradrenalin. Perhaps the most significant new discovery about stress is its suppressing effect on the immune system. Researchers have discovered that the body's production of its own cancer-fighting cells, including natural killer (NK) cells, T-lymphocytes and macrophages, is inhibited by chronic stress.

In late 1981, scientists at the Salk Institute synthesised the remarkable chemical that triggers the body's stress reactions. As mentioned previously, CRF is produced in the hypothalamus, a tiny but powerful structure sometimes called 'the brain's brain'.

Having duplicated CRF, the Salk scientists now hope to produce a modified version of the chemical that would actually block the body's reaction to stress.

It is accepted that stressors, including the disease, the diagnosis, the outlook, the treatment and the side effects, are there whether we like it or not. We also accept that such stressors reduce immune function *at the very time we want it to be soaring.* It is essential, then, to learn various strategies for addressing these and other everyday stresses in our lives.

Ten common rules of stress management

1. Set aside a time for reflection, meditation and relaxation.
2. Set goals and priorities and avoid conflicting goals.
3. Find support groups and rid yourself of negative influences around you.
4. Take care of your body.
5. Learn to manage and organise yourself and your time.
6. Don't worry about things that you can't control.
7. Dwell on your positive aspects and talents.
8. Learn how to say "NO".
9. Indulge in stress-free entertainment and hobbies.
10. Find solace and peace in your spiritual life.

What Actually Stresses You?

Ongoing stressful events/people/situations?

1.____

2.____

3.____

How do you cope? What do you do?

1.____

2.____

3.____

Stressful events/people/situations during the past week?

1.____

2.____

3.____

How did you cope? What did you do?

1.____

2.____

3.____

Five ways to examine stressful situations

1. Do you have some control over the stressor?
2. Is the stressor controlled by someone or something else?

3. Is it important to your life or professional goals?
4. Is it better to leave this alone?
5. Are benefits greater than the stress it will create to deal with the stressor?

Twelve ways to reduce stress

1. **Physical activity**: When you are nervous, angry or upset, release the pressure through exercise or physical activity. Running, walking, playing tennis, swimming or working in the garden are just some of the activities you can do. Physical exercise will relieve that uptight feeling and relax you. Remember, the body and mind work together! Even if you are capable of only tiny movements due to your condition, that is enough!

2. **Share your stress**: It helps to talk to someone about your concerns and worries. A friend, family member, teacher or counsellor can help you to see your problem in a different light. If you feel your problem is serious, seek professional help. Knowing when to ask will help you avoid serious problems later on.

3. **Know your limits**: If a problem is beyond your control and cannot be changed right now, don't fight the situation. Learn to accept it for the moment, until such time as you can take steps to change it.

4. **Take care of yourself**: You are special. Get enough rest and eat well. If you are irritable from lack of sleep or if you are not eating correctly, you will have less ability to deal with stressful situations. If stress repeatedly keeps you from sleeping, you should seek help.

5. **Make time for fun**: Schedule time for both work and recreation. Play can be just as important to your well being as work. You need a break from your daily routine to just relax and have fun.

6. **Be a participant**: One way to keep from becoming bored, sad, and lonely is to go where it is all happening. Sitting alone by yourself can leave you frustrated and lonely. Instead of feeling sorry for yourself, get involved and become a participant. Offer your services in Church, in the neighbourhood or volunteer

organisations. Help yourself by helping other people. Get involved in the world and the people around you, and you will find they will be attracted to you.

7. **Check off your tasks**: Trying to take care of everything at once can seem overwhelming and, as a result, you may not accomplish anything. Instead, make a list of the tasks you have to do; then do them, one at a time, checking them off as they're completed. Give priority to the most important ones and do those first. You don't have to finish the list.

8. **Must you always be right?**: Do other people upset you, particularly when they don't do things your way? Try co-operation instead of confrontation; it's better then fighting and always being 'right'. A little give and take on both sides will reduce the strain and can surprise you by making you both feel better.

9. **It's OK to cry**: A good cry can be a healthy way to bring relief to your anxiety, and it might even prevent a headache or other physical consequences. Take some deep breaths; they also release tension.

10. **Create a quiet scene**: You can't always run away, but you can 'dream the impossible dream'. A quiet country scene painted in your mind's eye or on canvas, can take you out of the turmoil of a stressful situation. Change the scene by reading a good book or playing beautiful music to create a sense of peace and tranquillity.

11. **Avoid self-medication**: Although you can use drugs to relieve stress temporarily, and they are a useful bridge to take you through a rough patch, they do not change the conditions that caused the stress in the first place.

12. **Learn the art of relaxation**: The best strategy is the method that works best for you.

The Stress Test

Holmes & Rahe Social Readjustment Scale

The scale lists forty-three common life changes in the order in which they have been found to be predictions of illness. To find your score, simply write in the values of the items in the following list that apply to you within the past year. Then add up your score and compare it with the range of scores that are given below the test.

Rank	Event	Value	Your Score
1	Death of spouse	100	________
2	Divorce	73	________
3	Marital problems	65	________
4	Jail term	63	________
5	Death of a close family member	63	________
6	Personal injury or illness	53	________
7	Marriage	50	________
8	Fired from work	47	________
9	Marital reconciliation	45	________
10	Retirement	45	________
11	Change in family member's health	44	________
12	Pregnancy	40	________
13	Sexual difficulties	39	________
14	Addition to family	39	________
15	Business readjustments	39	________
16	Change in financial status	38	________
17	Death of close friend	37	________
18	Change to different line of work	36	________
19	Change in no. of marital arguments	35	________
20	Mortgage or loan over £10,000	31	________
21	Foreclosure of mortgage/loan	30	________
22	Change in work responsibilities	29	________
23	Son or daughter leaving home	29	________
24	Trouble with in-laws	29	________

25	Outstanding personal achievement	28	________
26	Spouse begins or stops work	26	________
27	Starting or finishing school	26	________
28	Change in living conditions	25	________
29	Revision of personal habits	24	________
30	Trouble with boss	23	________
31	Change in work hours/conditions	20	________
32	Change in residence	20	________
33	Change in schools	20	________
34	Change in recreational habits	19	________
35	Change in Church activities	19	________
36	Change in social activities	19	________
37	Mortgage or loan under £10,000	17	________
38	Change in sleeping habits	16	________
39	Change in number of family gatherings	15	________
40	Change in eating habits	15	________
41	Vacation	13	________
42	Christmas season	12	________
43	Minor violation of the law	11	________
		Total	________

Total score less than 150:	37% chance of illness during next 2 years
150 to 300:	51% chance of illness
over 300:	80% chance of serious illness

Your Notes

The Doctor - Patient Relationship

The Patient Asks ...

Doctors and consultants... do please...

- Be careful of what you say. (A patient, recently tested, reported her consultant as saying "We didn't find too many *big* tumours this time...")

- If you're feel negative, please keep it to yourself (Remember, I hang on your on your every word!)

- Allow me to participate in the management of my illness.

- Do not think that you necessarily know all the answers.

- Allow me space to talk about complementary treatments I may have heard about. If, in your professional opinion, such treatments do not represent a risk to me nor will they interfere in my medical treatment, then allow me to make my own judgement.

- You have the skills and training to diagnose and to make a prognosis. I have the right to know what the worst **and** best case scenarios are. We, together, will determine where on that time scale I am likely to end up. (Please remember, nobody has the right to sentence me!)

The Doctor asks............

Patients do please ....

- Write your questions down (so you leave with the important ones answered). It's OK to give them to me written down. (Research shows a typical patient arrives with four to five questions, and leaves with less than two of them answered!).

- Obligations to other patients will probably limit the time I can give you to answer questions so prioritise your questions so the important ones are addressed first.

- Beware of **interpreting** a casual 'throw-away' comment. If you're not sure, ask!

- Do not pretend you understand if you don't. Ask!

- Make sure you understand the purpose of your medication, the dosage and frequency.

- Do report all unusual symptoms or possible side-effects. If necessary, write them down in advance.

- Your friends, family, or neighbours are not physicians or diagnosticians. Please do not rely on them for professional advice. If there is confusion, ask for clarification.

- Do not mix medications. Do not take natural/herbal/vitamins/minerals or OTC drugs without advising me. Even if I don't approve, I need to know! (Mega-doses of vitamins, minerals etc., can interfere with certain medications so check!)

- Do expect caring, respect, fairness and understanding.

- Communicate what you want and what your expectations are, and ask for as much information as *you* need.

- Do follow my prescriptions and recommendations. You are free to decline, but do, please, let me know!

- Feel free to ask for a second opinion.

- Feel free to ask (and if necessary, **insist on knowing**) "What's the longest anyone has survived with this illness with quality of life?" or "What's the shortest time anyone has taken to heal from this?" If I don't know, please ask me to find out!

- Do feel free to questions tests, their necessity and frequency.

Part 2

Interventions

Hypnosis and How the Mind Works

Hypnosis

Hypnosis is an altered state of awareness in which the unconscious accepts a suggestion which may well be at variance with what was previously believed. When people have been diagnosed, they are particularly susceptible to inadvertent hypnosis.

The Mind

The mind has been compared to an iceberg floating in the ocean, the small area above the water equating to the 'conscious' or 'thinking' part of the mind and the vast area beneath the water equating to the unconscious. For the purposes of this text, the unconscious is treated as **everything** outside of normal consciousness or awareness.

The Unconscious

The unconscious equates to a vast reference 'library' in which is stored every event, emotion and feeling from the moment of your birth. Wilder Penfield in 1969 won a Nobel prize for demonstrating that everything we experience is stored in the unconscious. Therefore, our reaction to new experiences is largely dictated by what we have experienced in the past.

Processing Capacity

The *conscious* mind is estimated to be capable of handling between five and nine tasks simultaneously. The central nervous system, however, is reported to be receiving up to 70,000 bits of information a minute! To be effective, the mind must therefore delete, distort and generalise virtually all incoming information so as to enable the conscious mind to think and concentrate and also must convert the received information into a format usable by the unconscious so it can know how to interact with the world at a later date.

Whenever the conscious mind encounters a request for information, 'researchers' are, in effect, dispatched into the 'library' of the mind to consult all relevant past 'files' in order to secure and deliver to you a way of responding or reacting to a given situation. The response delivered is not some form of sequential, digital stream of previous similar experiences but is a generalised, abbreviated, instantaneous 'answer'.

The Critical Factor

An important part of the mind is given the task of acting as 'critic' whose job is to appraise all incoming information and to select which beliefs, ideas, concepts, etc. are accepted into the unconscious or 'library' and, equally importantly, decide which ones are to be rejected. For instance, a person who accepted an overheard suggestion that 'the world is flat' might soon find themselves the subject of some derision?

In the context of counselling or hypnotherapy, we are seeking to install a **new** and more useful suggestion or belief system which often will be at variance with the 'status quo' as put forward by the 'librarians' in the unconscious ("You are an anxious person and that's how you are! Full stop! No discussion! We will accept no other contrary suggestions"). In this instance, the critic is an unwitting obstacle to change. In order to change or install an alternative program or more useful belief system, it is necessary to by-pass the critical part of the mind, and this where hypnosis and self-hypnosis prove useful.

Programming

The formula or recipe used for 'programming' or changing the mind is as follows:

Accepting Responsibility (A.R.) - (desirable)

\+ Relaxed Body (R.B.) - (desirable)

\+ Relaxed Mind (R.M.) - (desirable)

\+ Strong Emotion (S.E.) - (essential)

\+ Concentration (C) - (normally goes with the strong emotion)

\+ Suggestion (Sugg.) - (essential)

= Powerful Programming or conditioning

(thereby substantially by-passing of the critical factor!)

"If your receive a suggestion at the same time as you are experiencing a strong emotion, either positive or negative, that suggestion is likely to be accepted *without* the normal critical evaluation"

A person who has just received a diagnosis of a life threatening or 'quality of life' threatening disease is highly susceptible to suggestion from physician, family and friends alike. Words are often accepted like a 'hex' and can frequently make matters worse.

Timing of suggestion in relation to the experience of a strong emotion is critical. If the suggestion is made or imagined **just prior to** or **at the peak** of experiencing the strong emotion, an exponentially increased programmed response is brought about. If the suggestion is made after the peak of the emotional response, the programming effect will be fractional.

Intensity of Emotion
The strength or impact of programming is in direct proportion to the intensity of emotion experienced simultaneous with suggestion. The stronger the emotion, the stronger the programming.

Repetition
Where the strength of emotion involved is limited, repetition is used to compensate. Television advertising is one of the better examples of this principle.

Phobias as an example of Conditioning

Phobias provide us with an excellent example of the principles of hypnotic conditioning in action. The following is an actual case with certain details changed to protect confidentiality.

Female client flying from London, Heathrow to Malta on a surprise one-week Winter holiday with husband in January 1984

- Before her marriage, Client had flown many, many times over a number of years as an executive secretary with her employer. Flying was, therefore, a 'known entity'.

- Children and pets had been safely left with grandparents.

- Client and spouse had passports, money, hotel and car reservations and were looking forward to a lazy week in the sun. Client was now in a relaxed state (R.B.), sitting on the plane forty minutes out of Heathrow. She also had a relaxed mind (R.M.), perhaps internally making pictures of herself, sitting on the beach or by the pool, soaking up the warm sun and sipping a cool drink.

- Suddenly, the plane hits an air-pocket and drops abruptly. Coffee spills, people scream and the client experiences a strong emotion (S.E.): terror!

- Nearing the peak of this strong emotion (terror), she says to herself in her mind something like "The plane's going to crash, we're all going to die" and probably, simultaneously, creates or recalls pictures in her mind of previous aircraft disasters she may have seen on television or in the papers (Sugg.).

- The plane levels out, the coffee is mopped up and things are back to normal, or are they? In her conscious mind, she knows that flying is safe. She consciously knows this - because she's sitting in a plane! However, she has just gone through all the necessary steps for powerful conditioning: (R.B. + R.M. + S.E. + Sugg).

  Into her subconscious mind, without any 'critical judgement', there has crept a belief along the lines of "All planes crash!". Even though her actual suggestion was: "The plane's going to crash, we're all going to die!", the mind will generalise this into: "All planes crash!". She now experiences major conflict in the mind, the conscious mind saying: "Flying is safe" and, at the same time, the unconscious is saying: "All planes crash!". Whenever such conflict exists, the subconscious will always win, as it's a presupposition that 'everything' in the subconscious is 'correct'. It has already gone through critical evaluation or 'quality control'. Without this presupposition, a person would be unable to 'know' how to interact with his/her environment because they could not rely on the 'reference library'.

- The client returned from that holiday by boat and train and was unwilling to fly until she came for therapy in 1991. The phobia was successfully resolved.

The Wonder of a Phobic Conditioning

The person has developed a 'programming' or belief system which if left unresolved will probably last for life.

- In the above example, the time necessary to install this 'life' programme was approximately 30 seconds.

- The programming was based on 'synthetic' experience. In other words, the plane never crashed and nobody died. The subject simply imagined it vividly and in detail (the subconscious mind cannot differentiate between a real experience and one imagined vividly and in detail).

Note 1: Phobic response does occasionally dilute over time, generally due to informal but systematic desensitisation. This can occur through regular but distanced exposure to the feared object or event.

Note 2: This type of dysfunction-producing programming may lie dormant in the unconscious for years before manifesting. This is particularly distressing, as people frequently will have no conscious recollection of the original event, yet they can find themselves behaving or reacting irrationally, illogically, or in a manner completely at variance with their 'conscious' beliefs.

Your Notes

Hypnosis - Key Points

- Hypnosis is a relaxed state of 'altered' awareness) in which relatively rapid changes in behaviour or reaction may be brought about. It is not 'un-consciousness', a misleading impression sometimes given by stage entertainers.
- In hypnosis, you hear and, if you choose to, you remember everything.
- You are in full control at all times.
- You do not say anything you wouldn't normally say. You do not reveal secrets you would not normally openly discuss.
- You will not do anything you wouldn't normally do.
- Hypnosis is a GUIDED technique which can enable you easily to change some unwanted aspect of your life.
- Hypnosis is a 'state of concentrated attention and relaxation'.
- Hypnosis is choice. You choose the level; the therapist acts as a guide. You choose to follow the guided instruction.
- Hypnosis has a cumulative effect; every time you choose to enter a state of hypnosis, you can achieve a much deeper level.
- All hypnosis is self-hypnosis!
- Nothing is done which might embarrass you or cause discomfort.
- You cannot be left in a permanent state of hypnosis. If something were to happen to the therapist while you are hypnotised, you would drift into a deep sleep and wake up within minutes, feeling comfortable and refreshed.
- Just like driving a car, the things which can interfere with your being successful with hypnosis are:

  1) Excessive anxiety on your part (fear of losing control)
  2) Trying too hard
  3) Being excessively analytical about the process.

Behavioural Change Principles and Hypnosis

Effective remission or cure tends to come from a combination of the best of modern medicine and a **radical** change in lifestyle. Most people know **what** they should be doing, in terms of exercise, diet, stopping smoking, and thinking, but find it very difficult to actually know **how** to deliver the goods. Old habits and patterns get in the way. Also, when people are challenged or upset, they tend to resort to many of their least healthy behaviours, such as overeating, drinking and smoking, as a source of comfort. This is where professional counselling, hypnotherapy or psychological intervention can be helpful. Learning to develop skills with self-hypnosis and visualisation can also be a most effective way to enable a person to break through old habits and patterns.

It is essential that a 'fight-back' programme should include a review of such behaviour patterns as well as a **specific** and **timely** strategy for resolving them. If this is not done at a very early stage, future efforts will be constantly undermined

Conquering old, unwanted, habits is easier when we are ill, and tends to bring about a sense of pride and accomplishment which supports a 'taking charge' mind-set. Studies show that such mind-sets lead to improved immune function, faster recovery and better overall health.

Your Notes

Instruction Sheet for Learning Self-Hypnosis or Self-Programming

(Modified from the work of Dr David Spiegel)

1. Find somewhere quiet and comfortable.

2. Sit in a comfortable chair for a few moments and become aware of your breathing.

3. Pick a spot to focus on, just above your line of vision (**without** tilting the head).

4. Keeping the eyes **elevated**, allow the eyelids to close gently.

5. As soon as the eyelids close down, immediately take a long *deep* breath ... and then ... exhale **slowly** .... and as you do so, imagine the sensation of **floating** .... in the sea, in the bath, wherever .... and as you feel that, now, resting the elbow on the arm of a chair, begin to float your dominant hand upwards into a vertical position.

6. As you float the hand upward, begin repeating to yourself (in your mind) "My hand is floating up, my hand is floating up, my hand is floating ...." without interruption, until the hand is *vertical* (the purpose of this repetition is to keep the conscious mind occupied).

7. As soon as the hand is *upright*, offer an appropriate suggestion to yourself. Self-suggestions or programming should be stated positively (what you **want** rather than what you don't want). (see samples following....)

   Repeat your suggestion *twice,* allowing time for assimilation and where possible, visualising or imagining the results. Your objective is to make the goal *attractive* to the unconscious mind.

   (Work on *one project per session*. Prepare and write down or memorise your suggestion in advance! You may also open your eyes briefly to read your suggestion.)

8. When you've completed the suggestions, immediately take your mind back to the sensation of floating in the hand and now, start repeating to yourself (without interruption) "My hand is floating down, my hand is floating down, my hand is floating down...."

9. When the hand has returned to a relaxed position, open the eyes and allow yourself a few moments to re-orient.

Note: To learn the self-hypnosis technique correctly, it should be practised *at least 5-6 times a day* for 14 consecutive days. These training sessions take about 2 minutes from start to finish and should be *fun*. You are building a mental muscle!!!

Suggested times: 1. On rising, 2. Before leaving for school or work, 3. At lunch time, 4. On returning from work or school, and 5. Before going to sleep.

Reference: Trance & Treatment by Dr David Spiegel & Dr Herbert Spiegel, 1978. (1)

Sample Suggestions

Cancer: "My immune function is increasing in effectiveness by 10% each day"
"The cancer cells are weakening with each passing day"
"The chemotherapy/radiation therapy is destroying the cancer cells completely"
"The tumour(s) shrinks by 15% each day and will soon be gone"

Heart: "My coronary arteries are opening up by 10% each day"
"My heart is magnificent - it becomes more efficient with each passing day"
"My heart muscle is repairing and healing with every passing day"

Lupus/MS: "My immune system is now resetting itself to a healthy effective level"

Asthma: "My breathing becomes more calm and easy with each passing day"
"My lungs are more calm and effective with each passing day"
"I am now calm and relaxed and can breath easily and effortlessly"

Rheumatoid Arthritis: "My joints are becoming cooler and more flexible with every passing day"

Energy: "As I now care for my body and give it rest, my energy increases by 10% each day. I accept that there will be days when my body will want more rest and this is OK"

Stress: "I am becoming more calm and relaxed with each passing day"
"I now have the ability to push an inner 'pause' button when I feel myself becoming stressed"

Pain: "Pain is an important messenger. However, the discomfort I have been feeling is no longer necessary and decreases by 20% every day.

Nausea: "The treatment I'm receiving is highly effective. As I develop my ability to be calm and relaxed, the side effects become less and less"

Sleep: "As I develop my ability to relax each day, I now fall into a deep and peaceful sleep within a short time of lying down to rest"
"When I complete this self-hypnosis session, I will fall into a deep and restful sleep"

Fear: "My confidence in my body, its ability to heal and to make the best use of my medical treatment grows with each passing day"

Medication: "The tablets/treatment I'm taking become(s) stronger and more effective with every passing day"
"My body is learning how to use my medical treatment more effectively; I need less and less 'X' to produce the same effect"

(N.B. It is dangerous to change or reduce medication without consulting your doctor)

Meditation

Meditation is the process of quietening your mind. When your mind is quiet, you feel peaceful. Any sense of separateness and isolation from the world tends to disappear. Current research indicates that the regular practice of any one of a wide variety of meditation techniques can significantly improve the performance of your immune system, reduce stress and tension and improve the prospects of remission or cure. Researchers at the University of Miami found that daily meditation increased both the activity and numbers of immune cells. In a three-year study, involving residents of a nursing home, those who meditated were all alive at the end of the study as opposed to only 38% of the non-meditators.

Professor Herbert Benson at Harvard University has been carrying out clinical trials of meditation since the early 1970s, also showing measurable improvements. Jon Kabat-Zinn, PhD., has been running a hospital-based eight-week meditation programme at the University of Massachusetts Medical Centre for more than twenty years. Studies of his work show *reduced pain levels* and fewer side effects from treatment. In 1990, Dr Dean Ornish, a Harvard graduate cardiologist, was the first person to prove conclusively that *heart disease could be reversed;* his reversal programme includes meditation as a major component.

Meditation is now widely used to:

1. Improve immune function, the 'fight-back' system in the body.
2. Reduce the symptoms of illness.
3. Manage the side effects of treatment (tablets, chemotherapy, radiotherapy, surgery etc.)
4. Improve emotional well-being (become a nicer person to be around!)
5. Increase the likelihood of remission/cure.

The benefits of the technique are as follows:

- Relieves fatigue and helps you cope with subconscious anxieties.
- Reduces the stress that can lead to high blood pressure, hardening of the arteries, heart attack or stroke.
- Improves your ability to relax, both physically and mentally.

- Often reduces the frequency and/or intensity of headaches and also angina and arthritis pain.
- Useful in the treatment of lower back pain.
- Helps regulate cardiac arrhythmias.
- Reduces the severity of nausea/vomiting with chemotherapy.
- Reduces the tendency towards compulsive smoking, eating and alcohol abuse.
- Can help greatly with insomnia and sleep problems.
- Helps conserves the body's store of energy.
- Makes you more alert so you can focus on what's important.
- Often reduces cholesterol levels without the need for drugs.
- Can increase the HDL fraction in cholesterol.
- Improves immune function.
- Can be used anywhere, (train, bus etc.), even on the way to work.
- Can be learned in one easy session.
- Usable by anyone, regardless of age, religion or beliefs.
- Can reduce reliance on prescription drugs.
- Has no unpleasant side effects.
- No educational requirement or aptitude is necessary.

The Benson Medical Meditation Technique

The "Relaxation Response" is a simple, 'easy to learn', yet powerful form of private meditation. It was developed, during the early 1970s, by Dr Herbert Benson, M.D., a Professor of Medicine at Harvard Medical School and also Director of the Division of Behavioural Medicine and the Hypertension Unit at Boston's Beth Israel Hospital.

Instructions

1. Select a quiet calm environment with as few distractions as possible. Take the phone off the hook. Sit quietly and close your eyes, focusing on your breathing for a minute or two.

2. With your eyes closed, start repeating the word 'ONE' (or any other word or phrase of your choice) to yourself, silently or aloud. This repetition encourages the mind to desist from wandering and helps stem the constant train of distracting thoughts which normally pass through the mind. Breathe easily and naturally. Continue the

repetitions for fifteen to twenty minutes. You may open your eyes to check the time, but do not use an alarm. When you finish, sit quietly for a few moments, at first with your eyes closed and then with your eyes open.

3. Refrain from worrying about how well you are performing the technique. When distracting thoughts intrude (as they will), just gently let them pass on .... and return to the repetition of the word. This passive attitude is the most important element in producing the 'Relaxation Response'. Distracting thoughts will occur. When these thoughts do present themselves, and you become aware of them, just allow them to pass on. Simply return to the repetition of your chosen word. Refrain from worrying whether or not you are achieving a deep level of relaxation; this is not the objective. Maintain a passive attitude and *permit* relaxation to occur at its own pace. With practice, the response will come with little effort.

4. A comfortable upright sitting posture (not lying down) is important so that there is no undue muscular tension in your body. You should be comfortable and relaxed. Avoid crossing your legs or intertwining your fingers as this can interfere with blood circulation. Remember, when the body relaxes, its temperature will tend to fall slightly, so make sure you are in a warm environment with adequate clothing to maintain body temperature.

5. Practice the technique at least once (ideally twice) each day but not within two hours after any meal, since it has been shown that digestion interferes with the elicitation of the 'Relaxation Response'. Avoid, also, practising just before bed. When you finish, sit quietly for a few moments, at first with your eyes closed and then with your eyes open. When you stand up, do so slowly and gently.

Time Investment: 20 - 40 minutes a day

This is only one of a wide variety of meditation techniques that you could use. Many others are available and do not necessarily require allegiance to a particular faith. However, meditation forms an important part of Buddhist teaching, and it is perfectly possible to learn their particular techniques without becoming a Buddhist monk. Equally, in the last thirty years there has been a resurgence within the Christian Church, and the Catholic Church in particular, of meditation and contemplative prayer, largely as the result of the writings and teaching of Fr. John Maine.

You do *not* have to *like* meditation to derive benefit from it!

Optional Reading

Benson, Herbert, M.D. (1975), *The Relaxation Response*. New York: Avon Books. ISBN 0-380-00676-6.

Benson, Herbert, M.D., & Eileen Stuart, R.N. C.M.S., (1992), *The Wellness Book*. New York: Simon & Schuster. ISBN 0-671-79750-6

Goleman, Daniel, '(1988), *The Meditative Mind.* New York: Putnam Books. ISBN 0-87477-833-6.

Kabat-Zinn, Jon, Ph.D., (1991), *Full Catastrophe Living*, New York: Dell. ISBN 0-7499-1585-4

LeShan, Laurence, (1974), *How to Meditate.* London: Thorsons. ISBN 1-855382776-6 (13)

Your Notes

Visualisation/Positive Imaging

Visualisation is the process by which we form images or pictures in the mind's eye. As children we do this automatically. Many youngsters of five, six or seven will readily imagine their favourite TV programme, complete with imaginary screen, if it is suggested to them in the right way. As adults, we still visualise frequently as we process information, but visualising may, in some people, be unconscious for much of the time and needs a little time and practice to bring the mental pictures into conscious awareness.

Images are very useful and adaptable things, and can become a *representation* or *metaphor* for those parts of our bodies that are affected by an illness, for the illness itself and, even more importantly, for the means by which the body aims to heal itself. The following process will develop your own healing scenario, which may be accompanied by feelings and sounds too. Remember, as you do this, that the immune system is constantly eavesdropping on the scene.

A good example of this would be a person with arthritis visualising a special lubricant flowing into the joints to loosen them. A woman with breast cancer may see her tumour as, say, a field of grass, and her immune system as the sheep grazing on it, continually 'nibbling it away'. Others may like the metaphor of a battle, seeing their cancer as an enemy army and their immune system as soldiers in their own fighting force. The most important thing is to find a set of images that suits *you* and feels right for you.

How to Visualise

1. Sit down and make yourself comfortable.

2. Notice what your experience of your condition is *right now*, how you feel, what you see and what you hear in relation to it. Allow an image to come into your mind that represents the problem. This may be a simple image, say, of a blocked artery in the heart, or it may be a colour, a

shape, an object or a person which represents a cancer, a pain or any other symptom. Go with whatever comes up first - however bizarre it may seem.

3. Now *decide* what you want to have happen to this: arteries to open, pain to reduce, unwanted behaviour to change, tumour to shrink, etc., and note it down briefly.

4. Now decide what has to happen for the first image to become the second: a change in colour, shape or size; soldiers killing the enemy tumour cells - whatever is right for you. Do you need to add anything to the scene to help it change, or have you got enough resources present in the picture? If there is anything else you need, add it now. Now allow the change to occur until it is completely as you would wish.

5. Now close your eyes and go through a one minute body scan and relaxation session.

The One-Minute Relaxation

With eyes closed, take a deep breath, hold briefly and exhale slowly, then, take another breath and again hold, and exhale slowly. Each time you breathe in, imagine inhaling relaxation or some other 'good' feeling through your nostrils. Each time you exhale, flow that good feeling of relaxation, one by one, to different parts of the body as follows:

- The scalp and ears
- The head and face
- The neck and both shoulders
- The left arm and hand
- The right arm and hand
- The chest and abdomen

- The back muscles, upper, middle and lower
- The left hip and left upper leg,
- The left lower leg and left foot
- The right hip and upper leg,
- The right lower leg and right foot
- The entire body from the top of the head down to the tips of your toes.

(Note: Each time you do a one minute relaxation session, you are building a skill. Within a few weeks of regular practice, the body learns to do it in a matter of seconds so don't be surprised when you find it taking less and less time to relax!)

Visualisation can be done as part of your self-hypnosis routine but is not essential. Many patients working with visualisation use affirmations along with their internal imaging e.g. "The tumour is shrinking by 10 percent every day", My coronary arteries are opening up by 15% each week" etc.

Having relaxed, now form an internal image of what you want to change followed by an image of that change actually occurring. This should only take moments rather than minutes. Then return the focus to the body, breathe in, and as you exhale, send a wave of relaxation down through the body.

You should do at least two sessions of visualisation a day.

(Note: It is **not** essential to have crystal clear images in your mind. The research which has been done in this area found no differences in effect with those who were supposedly 'poor' imagers. Human being are unique in the way they represent things in their minds so however you do it is perfect! Just do it.

References/Resources

Simonton, Dr. O. Carl, & Matthews-Simonton, Stephanie, (1978). *Getting Well Again*. New York: Bantam. ISBN 0-553-17272-7.

Ornish, Dr. Dean, (1990). *Dr. Dean Ornish's Program for Reversing Heart Disease*. New York: Ballantine. ISBN 0-345-37353-7.

Relaxation Training Session

The following is the wording for a relaxation session which you can either record yourself onto tape or have someone read to you. It should be read at a steady relaxed pace with plenty of pauses (2 - 3 seconds) as indicated by the dots.

First of all, be sure that you are somewhere where you can be free of disturbance for at least 30 minutes. If possible, make things easy for yourself by perhaps taking the phone off the hook or hanging a '30 minute privacy' sign on the door. Remove your shoes or items of clothing that might interfere with your physical comfort in any way. As you will be relaxing and the body tends to cool when relaxing - perhaps cover yourself with a warm blanket, particularly in cold weather.

Relaxation Session

If you wish, lie down...... Make yourself comfortable and begin to relax. Now ..... just close your eyes. Please keep them closed until the session is finished..... With your eyes closed, (if sitting), place your feet flat on the floor..... Sit back firmly against the back of your seat, unclasp your hands and let them rest loosely in your lap. Make sure you are comfortable and warm.

Now, inhale slowly and deeply for a count of 5 ..... hold it for a count of 5 and.... then, exhale slowly ...... Now, inhale again for a count of 5, hold for a count of 5 and ... exhale again ..... slowly.

That's right now! ..... with your eyes closed ..... you can ..... begin to relax ..... though at first ..... you may..... be more aware of some things..... than you were before ..... because with your eyes closed..... it becomes easier and easier..... to become more and more aware ..... of a variety of things..... which otherwise might be overlooked ..... or perhaps even ignored. ..... Thoughts ..... your thoughts .... feelings ..... sensations ..... and the gradual alteration of awareness ..... as the mind begins to experience ..... that gradual letting go. ..... Letting go, perhaps ….. even of the effort ..... it takes to be aware ..... of exactly where your arms are positioned ..... or the hands ..... or fingers ..... and even the effort it takes ..... to be aware of which leg ..... left or right ….. might now seem to relax ….. more quickly or completely ..... than the other ..... may seem to be ..... relaxing now..... sometimes, too much effort to bother making...... However, it takes time to ….. experience that letting go. ….. In your own time …. in your own unique way ….. as you begin to…… learn ….. even more than before ….. about your own unique ability ….. to … relax ….. and let go ….. as the mind begins to flow ….. down ….. or perhaps even up ….. towards that place ….. of quietness and calm awareness. ….. A place of effortless relaxation …. and letting go ….. where ….. even the effort it takes ….. to be aware …. of the sound of my voice …. or the meaning of my words ….. may sometimes seem to be …. too much effort …. to bother making …..

It's so much easier simply to relax ….. and allow things to happen …. almost by themselves ….. A gentle drifting down ….. and a drifting back …. upwards ….. towards the surface of wakeful awareness at times ….. and that's fine too. …. This time belongs to you….. because you have a conscious mind ….. and an unconscious mind ….and that unconscious mind ….. the back of the mind ….. the part of the mind …. which has managed your health so successfully ….. until now ….. can …. hear ….. and understand ….. and respond …. to the things I may say … without the need for you to do anything at all ……. Right now, I don't want you to relax too deeply ..... or too soon ..... but sometimes ..... as you ….. go into a relaxed state ..... your body may twitch involuntarily ..... just like when you're about to ..... fall into a very deep deep sleep ..... and you will know ….. that it's only an indication ..... that you are entering ..... a very deeply relaxed state ..... and as you sit there ..... you can feel where your body is touching the chair ..... feel where your feet are ..... the temperature of the skin on your face ..... hear the sounds all around ..... sense the temperature of the room and ….. as you breathe, ... you may ….. feel your body settling ….. and relaxing very deeply now ….. down into the chair ..... and all the muscles ..... throughout your body

….. just begin to …..relax deeply now. So…..as you listen to the sound of my voice….. you may ….. choose to hear only my voice and ….. allow all other sounds to become unimportant .....

And now ..... focus your attention ….. on all the tiny muscles around your eyes ..... and if you concentrate carefully ..... and with certainty ..... you can ….. relax each and every one of these muscles NOW ..... and when you're sure these eye muscles ..... are completely and totally relaxed ..... so relaxed …. that you're sure ……they couldn't possibly open ..... even if you wanted them to …..allow that sense ..... or wave of gentle relaxation ..... to spread down into your cheeks ..... and when you are absolutely certain ..... your eyelids are so totally relaxed ..... that they wouldn't open ..... even if you tried ..... then try gently ..... and discover that they won't …. If they are completely relaxed ….. Your body is relaxing now ..... from the top of your head ..... all the way down ….. to the tips of your toes ….. and …… with each breath you breathe..... you may ….. find yourself ..... drifting even deeper ..... into a contented state ….. and now, ... feel that gentle wave of relaxation ..... continue to radiate ..... out from your eyes ..... into the cheeks ..... up around the ears ..... and perhaps, become aware ….. of a certain warm feeling in the ears ..... allowing the mouth to relax ... the tongue ... maybe even feel the jaw sag slightly ….. as it too relaxes ….. teeth separating ...... the throat ... the ears ... even the scalp becoming loose and limp ... feel the neck relaxing …..the sides of the neck ….. the front ….. the back ..... forehead smoothening out now ..... all those little imaginary frown and worry lines just disappearing ...... Now moving on down to the shoulders, almost like a warm blanket ..... send a wave of relaxation ….. down into the shoulders ... upper arms ... all the muscles in your arms now becoming loose and limp ... elbows ... lower arms ... wrists ... your hands relaxing now ... explore each individual finger ….. the back of the hands ... palms of the hands….. and any slight tingling sensation in the fingers is perfectly normal …. sometimes just a sign of the relaxation in your arms and hands….. and …… if you choose ..... you may ….. find that you are slowly drifting ..... still deeper and deeper ..... than you would ever have imagined possible ….. Now moving on down to your chest ….. feel that warm gentle wave of relaxation …… spread down over your chest and rib cage ….. the abdomen….. all the internal organs ..... beginning to settle and relax ..... and now ..... becoming aware of the muscles in your back, in the upper back, especially those big heavy muscles ... just like big rubber bands, loose and limp ….. the lower back ... the waist ..... all those muscles unwinding …… and relaxing ….. as you ….. become aware ….. of a growing sense of peace and contentment ….. Now, moving down to the hips, feel that wave of relaxation …... spread into the thighs…. front of the thighs …..the back of the thighs ..... the knees ... feel those calf muscles unwind... the ankles ….. the feet ... the soles of the feet ... the toes ..... and any slight tingling or light sensation in your toes ….. if it's there …. and only if it's there ….. it's perfectly natural and just a sign of the growing sense of relaxation …in the legs and feet. And now ..... without disturbing the relaxed state of your body ..... you may …. notice ..... in a somewhat detached manner ..... the fact that ..... with each breath you breathe in ..... you feel the relaxation spread ..... to every corner of your body ..... and ..... with each breath you exhale ..... you may notice ..... how you are expelling any remaining stresses ..... or tensions ..... totally from your body ..... and this allows your body ..... to relax even further ..... and still deeper ..... into relaxation….. Feel that gentle wave of relaxation .... washing from the top of your head, ... all the way down ….. to the tips of your toes….. All the muscles and tendons, unwinding and relaxing….. Each time you inhale, you can ….. imagine breathing in relaxation. ….. Each time you exhale ..... you can explore ….. flowing a wave of relaxation ….. from the top of your head ..... all the way down to the tips of your toes….. and as you continue to listen ..... to the sound of my voice ..... and explore a sense of warmth …..spreading throughout the body ..... as it continues to settle, ... you may …..choose to drift ..... even further and deeper still ..... towards a profound state ….. of peace and contentment ..... maybe twelve times deeper than ever before ..... and you may become aware ….. perhaps for the first time ..... of the colour …… or texture ….. or sound ..... of deep relaxation ..... and know ..... that this can be any colour ..... or texture ..... or sound that you choose ….. and also knowing ..... with certainty .....

that you can have this state ..... any time or place you choose. In a moment I will count backward from 10 to 1. ...... As I count backwards.... if you wish ..... you will ..... continue to drift deeper and deeper into relaxation ..... deeper than you have ever been before.

See the number '10' now clearly in your mind

.. DEEP now ...... into relaxation

9 deeper still ......

8 ......

7 ..... continuing to go so deep into relaxation

6.....

5 .....

4 ..... deeper and deeper still

3 ......

2 ......

and finally ....1.....

Exploring gentle warm waves of relaxation ..... washing through you now .... a little more so ...... with each time you practice this process ..... exploring ..... in your own unique way ..... a sense of ..... being relaxed ..... muscles becoming loose and limp ..... unwinding ..... feeling peaceful ..... calm ..... tranquil ..... safe ..... warm ..... almost like you are floating ..... in a tiny white sailboat ..... on an imaginary lake of tranquillity..... feeling peaceful ..... letting go ..... drifting ..... drowsy ..... breathing so slowly now.

Remembering ... that relaxation is a learned skill ... and each and every time you choose to ... explore this state of relaxation .... you succeed .. in being able to go ..... much deeper than before ..... and ..... enjoy the feelings and sensations even more.

Right now ..... I'd like to invite you ….. to ….. go back into your past ..... and find there ….. some pleasant memory ..... of a relaxing time or place ..... that perhaps, you haven't thought about ..... for a while ..... and I'd like to invite you ..... that's right selecting just one such memory now ….. to ….. float inside that memory ..... as though ….. you are there right now ….. and begin to ….. become aware ..... of what you can see (pause eight seconds). ..... In your mind's eye, look around and notice what you can see ….. and also, …. become aware ..... of the sky ..... the temperature ..... and perhaps explore ….. even the tastes or feelings inside that memory ….. as though … you are there right now ..... because inside that memory ..... is enjoyment for your conscious mind. ..... This is a special place in your mind ..... where you can ….. experience contentment and relaxation ..... and each time you ….. choose to return there ..... in your mind ..... you may ….. experience just a little more .... and ….. it may be something you hear ..... it may be something you see ..... you may even meet somebody ….. who brought you happiness ...... in the past ..... and as you continue to be aware of your breathing ..... and the movement of your chest ..... each breath carries you ….. still deeper ….. into a very pleasant state of relaxation

Allowing that gentle warm waves of relaxation ….. to wash through you now …. even more …… with each occasion ….. you practice this process ….. exploring ….. again ….. in your own unique way ….. this sense of ….. feeling relaxed ..... muscles loose and limp ..... unwinding ..... feeling peaceful ..... calm ..... tranquil ..... safe ..... warm ..... almost like you are floating ….. like being in a tiny white sailboat ….. on an imaginary lake of tranquillity..... feeling peaceful ..... letting go ..... drifting ..... drowsy ….. breathing so slowly now.

Now ..... take a moment ..... to wander back …. through your personal history …. but this time …… at the unconscious level ….. and if you're not sure how to do that ….. just imagine that you do ….. allowing your unconscious ….. time to identify some resource … which can now be of use to you ….. in dealing with the present challenge.

….. It's not necessary for you to identify that resource with the conscious mind. ….. or ….. you might allow your unconscious ….. to present you with some dream or memory from the past ….. which you can enjoy ….. but I know ….. that if and when you begin that dream or memory from the past ….. Its only important that you learn …. and you learn ….. exactly what you need to know... What both you and I want is….. for your unconscious mind …… to bring about the changes you want …… without you even knowing what you've done at all.

To ensure you can …… have a sense of relaxation whenever you wish …… I'm going to offer you a means of recapturing …… and perhaps intensifying the sense of peace and control over your life which you are developing.

If and whenever you begin to feel any sense of stress or are feeling unresourceful, allow your mind to drift automatically …… to some resourceful or pleasant moment, and begin to ….. access your sense of calmness and relaxation. …… Now, inhale …. and ….. as you do so, imagine ….. you are inhaling ….. even more relaxation through the nose ….. and as you exhale ….. flow that feeling down through your body … from the very top of your head ….. all the way down ….. to the very tips of the toes …… and, as you do that, allow that sense of calmness, that sense of control ….. to just become stronger ……. and stronger ……. and even stronger and …… and …… when you have a sense …. that …… it has become as strong as it can be to-day …… joining the thumb and little finger of your left hand together …. and applying just a little gentle pressure …… now ….. inhale through the nose and ….. in your mind …. say the words "***calm and in control now***" to yourself.

This simple action will allow you to trigger the return of the feelings of control and relaxation which you are feeling now.

Pleased with yourself that you are taking these first steps in regaining complete control of your life. You are now .... free to discover ..... that when you get up to-morrow morning ..... and for many, many mornings to come ..... that you have the beginnings ..... of even more vitality and energy. ..... This increase in energy and vitality may develop slowly at first but every day ..... will see an increase.

When you open your eyes later on, you will ...... feel as though you've had a pleasant rest and ..... unless it's particularly important...... your conscious mind may ..... decide to remember very little of what has been said during this session ..... but you will know ..... that something interesting has begun and ..... that the changes you want .... will continue to evolve during the coming weeks and months.

Take a few moments now ...... to float back into your past ..... to find again that pleasant memory ...... of a special place or time ...... that you perhaps you hadn't thought about ...... for a long time ...... and ..... become aware again of the sights and sounds .... Take that time...... and I'll be quiet for that time ..... to allow you to enjoy it (be quiet for 30 seconds) ......

And as you are .... in that place, you can ..... know that you have trained well to-day ..... and lots of things have become activated ..... at the unconscious level ..... which are useful for you in a positive way...... Over the coming days and weeks ..... you ..... notice understandings emerging from your unconscious mind..... As a result of the many things you are doing ..... to support your body's natural ability to ..... recover healthfulness..... you ..... notice changes ..... alterations in your reactions and responses ..... all of which come as a delightful surprise for you...... And now, as you ..... gather back into yourself ..... all the parts of yourself ..... that have expressed themselves in your mind ..... during this relaxation training session, you can ..... sense the energy that they represent ..... now made available to your unconscious mind..... to continue the processes you've begun here ..... in a meaningful way ..... long after you've opened your eyes.

Take a few moments now to …… prepare yourself to wake up

In a moment, I'll count from 1 - 5 and as I do, you gradually return to full focused awareness …..feeling energised ….. perhaps having learned things …… which …. you may or may not choose to remember …. but which are changing your life ….. in the way that you want.

1 ….You are beginning to awaken now.

2 …. You are relaxed from head to toe …all your body functions moved to an optimum state.

3 …… Physically you are ….. feeling light ….. emotionally elevated ….. exceptionally clear headed.

4 ….. Happy with all you are planning in your life.

5….. You are WIDE AWAKE NOW.

Your Notes

Yoga

Bodies heal less rapidly and less completely when they are not cared for. Dr. Jon Kabat-Zinn, of the University of Massachusetts Medical Centre, describes Hatha Yoga as an ancient discipline of "gentle stretching and strengthening exercises, done very slowly, with moment to moment awareness of breathing and of the sensations that arise as you place your body into various configurations known as postures". Unlike most exercise or aerobic classes which focus on push-push-push, yoga is available to anyone, and research is showing it to be a very powerful adjunct to any healing programme.

Reasons for the Practice

Dr Dean Ornish demonstrated in 1989 that it is possible to reverse heart disease using yoga, meditation and group work. Dr Jon Kabat-Zinn has been running the stress programme at the University of Massachusetts Medical Centre for more than fourteen years using yoga and meditation as the key components. Studies of his work have shown measurable clinical improvements with medical patients with such diverse conditions as heart disease, cancer, lung disease, hypertension (high blood pressure), headaches, chronic pain, seizures, sleep disorders, stress related digestive problems and skin problems, to name just a few.

Apart from the encouraging clinical medical evidence which is now emerging, yoga as an adjunct to standard medical is attractive because:

- It is *user friendly* and can be practised lying, sitting, in a wheelchair or in bed.
- All that needed is that you are breathing and *some voluntary movement* is possible.
- *Any age-group* can work with yoga.
- It is suitable for *virtually all medical conditions.*
- It is *accessible* with courses (with trained teachers) available virtually every where.
- *No prior knowledge,* training or fitness capability is needed.
- It is **gentle** and progressive.

Myths

For many years, people have been fascinated by pictures of Indian yogis twisting their bodies into strange and exotic poses. These people will have spent many years of training and usually practice yoga for 2-3 hours a day. This has *absolutely nothing* to do with the practice of yoga for therapeutic purposes as part of a 'fight-back' programme.

The Effects of Yoga Practice

- Increases mindfulness
- Increases sensitivity or awareness in the body
- Increases flexibility
- Improves sleep patterns
- Stimulates and improves the function of the internal organs
- Develops breathing & lymph function
- Enhances immune function
- Reduces pain
- Increases awareness of eating, food quality and quantity
- Changes attitude to a more hopeful one
- Reduces depression and increase sense of well-being

Key Points

- You may start at *any level of wellness,* fitness or proficiency. If all you can do is lift your hand one inch to-day, hold it there mindfully, and then relax it, that is more than enough!

- Your objective is to move into a 'posture', hold in that position mindfully for a few seconds and then release and allow the posture to integrate.

- Your objective is to stretch into a pose to the point of **mild challenge** or discomfort, hold **mindfully** and then release.

- If you push yourself too far, you will probably either give up or at the very least, retard your progress.

- 15-20 minutes a day is all it takes.

- If you go to a weekly class. you're more likely to stick with practice. Also, working with a sociable group actually improves immune function. Make sure your yoga teacher knows what your condition is and what you're seeking to do. It's a mistake to be secretive about your condition!.

- The regular practice of yoga sends an important message to the immune system.

Getting Started
The easiest and most useful way to learn yoga is with a trained teacher. The Irish Yoga Association (or any national association) can provide lists of teachers. Keep in mind that few, if any, of these teachers are trained to work specifically with medical conditions, but that should not discourage you. Discuss it with your doctor, and advise your yoga teacher about your condition. Also, most bookshops have excellent straightforward books on the subject but do stick to a *beginners' level* book.

The following illustrations show a selection of postures which you may care to explore keeping the above principles in mind. Do remember that an illustration or picture is something to *move towards*, and is *NOT* something you have to achieve to-day. Remember, if all you can do to-day is lift one finger mindfully, hold it for a moment and then allow it to relax, that's perfect. You've started!

Starting today, incorporate 15 - 20 minutes of gentle stretching (with awareness) into your daily routine. Ask a teacher to design a specific programme for you.

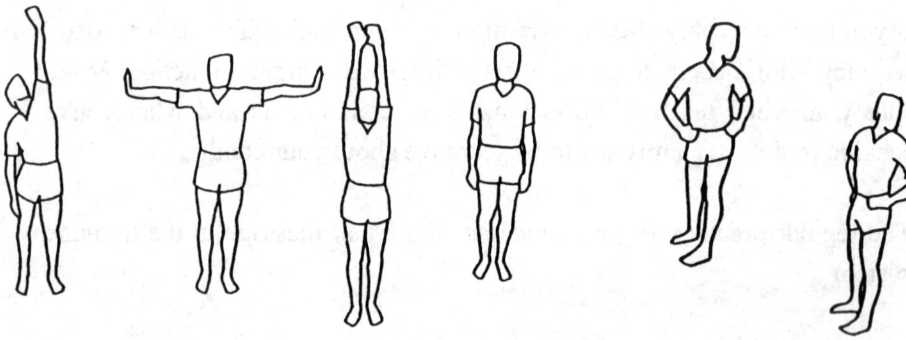

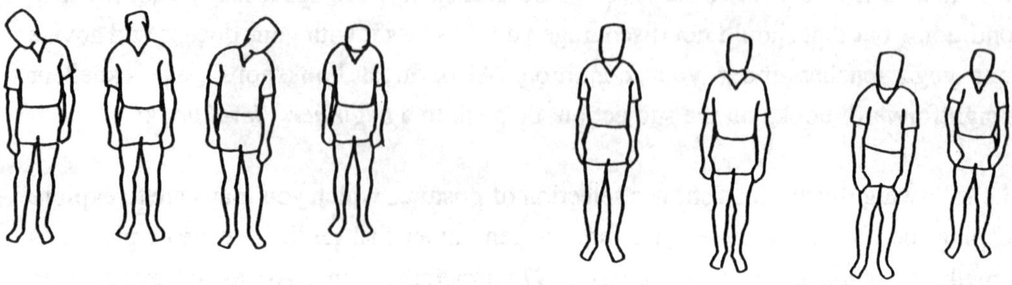

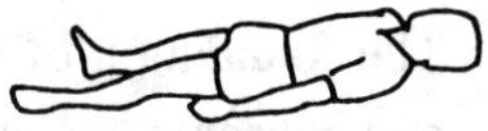

Breath Training

Without food, we die in months; without water, days; without air, we die in minutes. We need air to oxygenate our blood to in order to oxygenate the cells from which we are made.

The foundation of health is a healthy bloodstream, the system that transports oxygen and nutrients to every cell in your body. If you have a healthy circulatory system, you will live a long and healthy life. The key element for that system is breathing. It's the way you oxygenate the body and stimulate the life processes of each and every cell. Breathing not only controls the oxygenation of the cells, it also controls the flow of lymph fluid, containing the white blood cells which are a major player in the immune system, the defence mechanism of the body.

The lymph system is sometimes described as the body's sewage system. Every cell in your body is surrounded by lymph. You have four times as much lymph fluid in your body as you have blood. Blood is pumped from your heart through your arteries to the tiny porous vessels called capillaries. The blood carries oxygen and nutrients to the capillaries, where they are then diffused into this fluid around the cells called lymph. The cells, having an intelligence for what they need, absorb the oxygen and nutrients necessary for their health and then they excrete toxins, some of which goes back into the capillaries. Dead cells, blood proteins and other toxic material must be removed by the lymph system. This lymph system is activated by deep breathing.

The body's cells depend on the lymph system as the **only** way to drain off the large amounts of toxic materials and excess fluid which can restrict the amount of oxygen available to the cells. The fluid passes through the lymph nodes where dead cells and all other poisons (except blood proteins) are neutralised and destroyed. The lymph system is important, because if it were to shut down for twenty four hours, you would be dead as the result of blood proteins and excess fluid being trapped around the cells.

The bloodstream has a pump - your heart. However, the lymph system doesn't have one. The only way lymph moves is through deep diaphragmatic breathing and muscular movement. Think of what you do when you wake up after a snooze? You may stretch, you may yawn and will often take a deep breath to shake off the feeling of weariness. If you want to have a healthy bloodstream with effective lymph and immune systems, it is essential to develop the ability to breath deeply to produce the physical movements that will stimulate them effectively.

Be wary of any 'health programme' that doesn't first and foremost teach you how to fully cleanse your body through effective breathing.

Dr. Jack Shields, a highly regarded Lymphologist from Santa Barbara California, conducted an interesting study of the immune system. He placed miniature cameras inside people's bodies to see what stimulated cleansing of the lymph system. He found that a deep breath, from the diaphragm, is the best and most effective way, creating something like a vacuum that sucks lymph through the bloodstream and multiplies the pace at which the body eliminates toxins. It has been shown that deep breathing and exercise can accelerate this process by as much as fifteen times!

An understanding of the importance of deep breathing can dramatically increase the level of your body's health, which is why health systems like yoga focus so much attention on healthy breathing and muscle stretching and releasing.

Dr. Otto Warburg, Nobel prize winner and director of the Max Planck Institute for Cell Physiology, studied the effect of oxygen on cells. He was able to turn healthy cells into malignant cells simply by lowering the amount of oxygen available to them. This research has been replicated many times since.

What does this tell us? The researchers came to believe that lack of oxygen seems to play a major role in causing cells to become malignant or cancerous. It certainly affects the quality of life of the cells.

Remember that the quality of your health depends on the quality of the life of your cells. Thus, fully oxygenating your system would seem to be a number one priority, and breathing effectively is certainly the place to start.

One in three people will die from cancer. Athletes, however, experience only one case of cancer to every seven in the general population. Why? The suggestion is that athletes are giving the bloodstream its most important and vital element - oxygen - and triggering their bodies' immune system to work at maximum levels by stimulating the movement of lymph through physical activity. The problem for most of us is that we just don't know how to breathe!

There is no one perfect method for breathing. However, if you're planning to fight back against illness efficiently, here is one method which enhances diaphragmatic breathing. Any trained medical person, health coach or yoga teacher will also be able to teach you methods to enhance your breathing, so as to improve the efficiency of your lymph system.

The 1:4:2 Method - How to Breathe

For a count of ten breaths, breathe in the following ratio: inhale for one count, hold for four counts, exhale for two counts. So if you inhaled for three seconds, you would hold for twelve and exhale for six.

When you exhale for twice as long as you inhale, that's when you eliminate toxins via your lymphatic system. When you hold for four times as long, that's when you can fully oxygenate the blood and activate your lymphatic system. When you breathe, you should start from deep in your abdomen, like a vacuum cleaner that's getting rid of all the toxins in the blood system.

As part of your 'fight-back' programme, you might explore taking ten such breaths in the above ratio on **at least three** separate occasions a day.

Again, starting in the abdomen, take a deep breath through your nose while counting to three, (or pick a larger or smaller number based on your ability). Hold your breath for a count of twelve (or four times that of your inhalation). Then exhale slowly through your mouth for a count of six (or twice the length of your inhalation). You should never strain yourself. See what numbers you can build up to by **slowly** increasing the number and frequency of these sessions.

Always breathe to match your present capability. Do not strain. If breathing in for a count of one, holding for four and exhaling for two is all that you can do to-day, that's perfect! You've made a good start.

Qi Gong - Chinese method for stress management

1. Sit on the front edge of a straight-backed chair - feet flat on the ground, shoulder width apart.

2. Hold the spine straight, but not rigid. Hold the head level.

3. Soften the shoulders and let your hands rest lightly on your knees, palms facing upwards.

4. Relax the chest.

5. Breathe softly and slowly through the nose, creating an awareness of the breath coming into a point in the centre of the chest. Feel this breath sinking from the chest down down to the lower abdomen, and continue this feeling with each outward breath. Whilst continuing to breathe softly, being aware of your breath travelling between the chest and lower abdomen, get a feeling of all the tension in your neck and shoulders flowing down your arms and out through your upturned palms.

6. At first, take at least five minutes, or more if it's comfortable for you. (As you become accustomed to this practice, you can do it for about 20 minutes or more each day.)

7. To finish the session, take your arms (palms still facing upwards - gathering energy from the air), out to your sides and over your head, fingers not quite touching. Then continue the movement of the hands down in front of the face, bringing the energy down in front of your body to lower abdomen.

8. Hold the final position for some moments to experience this energy.

Adapted by Gary Collins, TCM Practitioner, specialising in Qi Gong and T'ai Chi Chuan

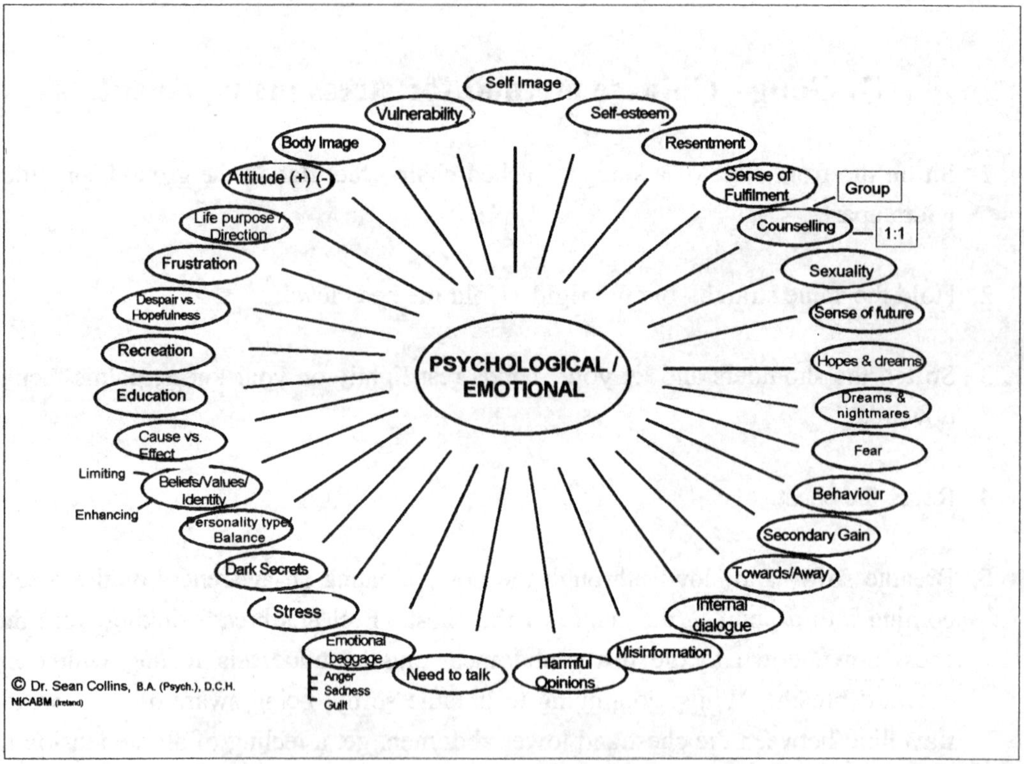

15. **Psychological/Emotional**: *The many, many aspects of 'self' which will impact upon your body and your prognosis, either positively or negatively. You choose!*

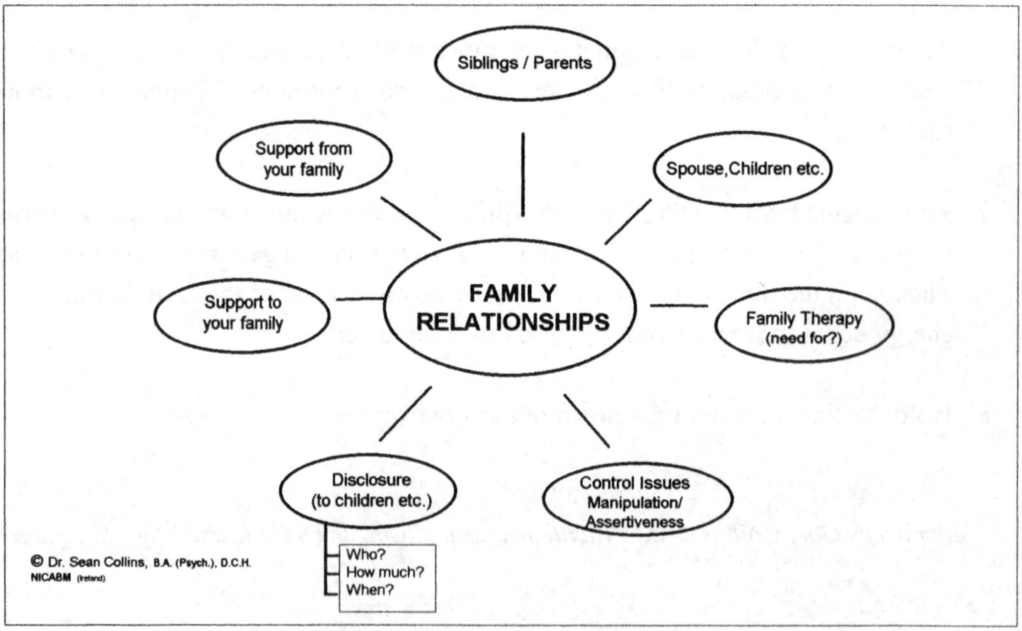

16. **Family Relationships** ***The Family*** *as a source of* ***toxicity*** *or* ***support****. Aspects for consideration*

Journalling

Dr James Pennebaker has been studying the relationship between physical and psychological well-being and the 'ability' to share feelings. His research revealed that *repressing* negative emotions, such as anger, fear, hurt, or guilt, promotes unhealthy conditions in the body and that the *expression of feelings,* especially through writing, has a measurable and *significant effect* on immune function. This effect lasts long after the writing has ceased, as shown by increased numbers of T cells (white cells in the body which are known to fight cancer and infections) and generally better health.

In Ireland, the practice of regular confession amongst Catholics has fallen away in recent years. From the perspective of Pennebaker's work, this form of expression was helpful and healthful for people.

The Pennebaker Process

Do you have emotional 'baggage' it would be useful to be rid of ? Do you want to stimulate your immune function?

By writing a journal of a particular traumatic event or series of events, detailing not only what happened, but also our feelings about it; a change takes place. As new insights are gained, an event which once triggered strong negative emotions is seen in a different light, and a feeling of neutral acceptance develops.

- Allow twenty to thirty minutes daily over four to five consecutive days.
- Find somewhere quiet and relaxing where you won't be disturbed.
- Start writing about the event or series of events that are most significant to you - this may relate to any time in your past, from birth to now. Write about your 'secret' or any theme relating to this.

- Keep going for at least twenty minutes. Even if you have run out of things to write about, write about that!
- Stop after thirty minutes. You may have much more to write, but there is always tomorrow.
- Repeat the following day, for a total of four or five days.
- If other events come up, note them down - then leave them. You can come back and repeat this process, but stay with one event or theme at a time.
- Make sure you write both the facts and the emotions or feelings you experience:

  a) at the time, and
  b) from today's perspective

The process may be irritating or annoying at first. Do NOT worry about grammar, spelling, composition or sentence structure. Discuss your deepest thoughts and feelings. Write about any subject ... ideally the one you may have kept private or secret. Allow the story to unfold rather than construct it. The sequence and order is not important. It is critical to let go and touch your deepest emotions and thoughts.

There is no 'RIGHT' way to do this process.

Dr Pennebaker observes that "this form of writing does **not** necessarily help a person to feel better right away. In fact, the individual may feel *more* anxiety or depression for a while; however as insights are reached, the bad feelings lift dramatically. Things may get worse before they get better - but they always get better if you persist".

As you proceed through the week, other traumatic or emotional events may come up. Just keep a note of them for another time and then continue. Your objective is to neutralise ONE event or period.

Keep your notes in a private place. It is **not** useful to read over your notes. However, do consider reviewing your writings with a professional counsellor or therapist as this too has been shown to enhance immune function increases.

Process Author: Dr. James Pennebaker, Ph.D.(Southern Methodist University, Dallas)

Letting Go of Negative Emotion

Our personalities are frequently dominated by some particular 'negative' emotion such as anger, sadness, fear, hurt or guilt - it's almost as though that emotion has become the dominant feature in our lives. All of us know people who, much of the time, display negative, depressed, timid or angry personality traits. From a psychological standpoint, what tends to cause this is a long history of *occurrences,* involving that particular emotion, being stored at the unconscious level *without the emotions being resolved.* For that person, when even a trivial event occurs involving that particular emotion, it will tend to trigger the release of **all** the old emotions attaching to similar events from the past. Ordinary everyday emotions such as anger can then become sudden rage, sadness can become depression, and fear can become extreme anxiety or timidity.

Extremes of particular negative emotions have become identified with particular diseases, e.g. anger has become associated with heart disease, and guilt and depression with cancer. In seeking to tip the balance in the direction of health the release of repressed negative emotions is essential. However, the typical life-challenged person does not have the time available to engage in counselling or therapy requiring, perhaps, many months or even years for resolution.

A number of psychological procedures have been developed which can, if the patients wishes, enable them to release negative emotion at the unconscious level in a matter of five to six hours **without** having to explore each and every past related event. TimeLine Therapy, developed by Dr. Tad James, is an example of such a process. This type of intervention is best done with a qualified psychologist, therapist or counsellor but is worth the effort.

Reference: *Time Line Therapy and the Basis of Personality* by Dr Tad James and Wyatt Woodsmall, 1988, Meta Publications, ISBN 0-916990-21-4

Prayer

Clients I work with bring a whole range of religious belief systems with them ranging from agnosticism to deep faith. On a personal note, I do remember that the coronary care unit tended to have fewer agnostics than one might meet outside in the street. When a person is life-challenged, he is more likely to remember the old maxim "In times of trouble, man remembers his God" The question is however, does prayer actually work?

In 1988, Dr. Randolph Byrd explored the effects of intercessory prayer on heart patients in San Francisco General Hospital's cardiac care unit. His research was a randomised, controlled, double blind prospective study involving nearly 400 patients over a six month period. As patients entered the cardiac care unit, they were randomly allocated to one of two groups. Approximately half were assigned to a group (Group A) to be prayed for by prayer groups, of differing denominations, up to 300 miles away, and the other half were assigned to a group (Group B) which was *not* remembered in prayer. For each patient in Group A, five to seven people in various locations prayed for that individual, being aware only of his or her name and medical condition. Group A turned out to be five times less likely to require antibiotics, three and a half times less likely to experience pulmonary oedema, and none of the prayed-for groups needed artificial airways, whereas 6% of Group B needed them.

Other similar studies have been carried out by researchers, such as Dr Larry Dossey, an internal medicine specialist, showing similar promising intriguing possibilities. However, this type of research remains controversial because there is no clear scientific explanation for the results produced and there are frequent inconsistencies in results.

However, if you or someone you care about is seeking to tip the balance, to remove the 'one straw from the camel's back' so that it's no longer at risk of breaking, then, regardless of your own religious views, can you afford to exclude prayer for self or others from the equation?

Diet and Fuelling

(How, what, when, where - vitamins, minerals etc.)

The human body is extremely adaptable. The way we normally eat when we are in the fullness of health is challenging enough for the body: rushing meals, not chewing, being absorbed in TV, eating in anger, sluicing food down with copious amounts of beer, wine, water, tea or soft drinks. As far back as the 1900's, Franz Mayr, a German physician, developed a method of eating which proved to be helpful in assisting the body to detoxify itself and to render the entire process of digestion **less stressful** to the physical system. A person who is health-challenged and who is seeking to trigger a healing response in the body will usually benefit enormously from 60 - 90 days of optimum eating.

Before you look at the guide-lines, do remember these are guide-lines and NOT instructions. They are *principles to aim at,* knowing the more you can implement these, the greater the effect you will produce.

Guide-lines for Optimum Feeding of the Challenged Body

A. How to eat

1 Take enough time - **at least 30 minutes** for meals.

2 Serve foods that are **attractive** to look at and to eat.

3 Eat **slowly**, in comfort and leisure.

4 Take **small bites.**

5 **Chew** carefully and ensalivate every bite until food is liquid. (diagrams of the human digestive systems generally include the mouth!) Food well chewed is food already half digested!

6 Savour each bite and **eat mindfully**. (As an experiment, take a single raisin and place it in your mouth **mindfully**. For about a minute, just roll it about in

your mouth **without chewing it** or swallowing it. Muse on the raisin itself, the country it came from, the soil from which it drew nourishment, the vine upon which it grew, the workers who tended it and transported it, the sun that shone on it, the rain that gave it moisture. Now for about two minutes, actually chew the raisin **without swallowing**. Under no circumstances swallow until the two minutes are up. Have fun!)

7 Concentrate on your eating. You are providing **fuel** for your body. Free yourself from distractions and disturbances (newspaper, conversation, television, radio etc.) Actually focus on what you are doing.

8 If you use dentures, make sure that they fit and that the bite is aligned.

9 'Chew' all your liquids. Ensure that all liquids have been mixed with saliva **before swallowing.**

10 Large volumes of **liquids should not be taken with meals** as they tend to dilute the digestive juices in the stomach and add an avoidable 'stress' element. If you're desperate, tiny sips of water, well chewed, are permissible. In a short time, the body rediscovers the ability to produce saliva.

B. When to eat

The body carries out much of its own repair work at night as we sleep. However, it takes 8-12 hours for the bulk of a meal to pass through the digestive system. Have you ever noticed how you feel on waking, having had a very heavy meal the previous night?

A large proportion of the energy in the food you eat is actually utilised in the process of digestion. Therefore, if you want to make things easy for your body in self-repair, eat your **main meal at midday,** so that when you lie down to sleep at night, your digestion is essentially finished and the body can concentrate on repair and renewal.

C. What to eat

Subject to instructions from your physician or nutritionist, you should eat a variety of foods on the basis that a ***little*** of what you fancy is good for you. The jury is long since back on the theory that fats and sugars put stress on the body. If you want to minimise the stresses on the body during your recovery, you should follow the guide-lines of the heart and cancer societies world-wide: this includes minimising the amount of meat, dairy produce, sugar and fat that you consume, and maximising on complex carbohydrates such as potatoes, bread, pasta and rice, with moderate amounts of fish and a wide variety of fruit, vegetables, pulses and nuts.

Note: Success depends on *consistent adherence!* Its what you do *daily* that counts!

D. Water

People who are ill frequently become dehydrated without even noticing. Through our natural eliminations, faeces and urine, we lose water. In addition, we lose it through perspiration and even breathing. When we are taking chemotherapy, potent medications, or perhaps experiencing 'night sweats', the body needs even more. Lack of water inhibits the immune system. The environment your cells live in is not blood, it is fluid called lymph. The lymphatic system requires adequate supplies of water to function at its best. Our bodies are ninety per cent composed of water. We can live without food for perhaps sixty to ninety days, provided we have access to water. Without water, the kidneys pack up and we die in five to ten days. Water helps the body to flush out toxins and residues from medical treatment. If you don't keep a regular flow of water through the drains at home, what happens? They clog! The human body is no different. Ensalivate all liquids rather than swilling them down; sip rather than sluice! Drink at least eight glasses per day of high quality water.

Note: These guide-lines are not necessarily for the rest of your life. They are essential only if you are seeking to offer your body an absolute *optimum healing environment.*

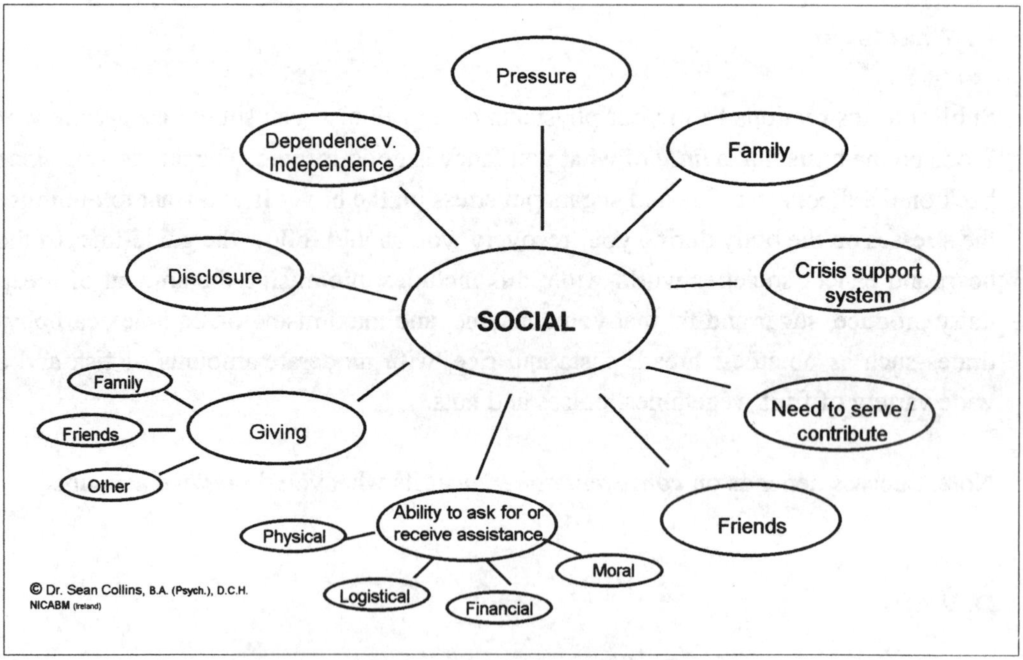

17. **Social:** *An overview of potential support structures and items for consideration*

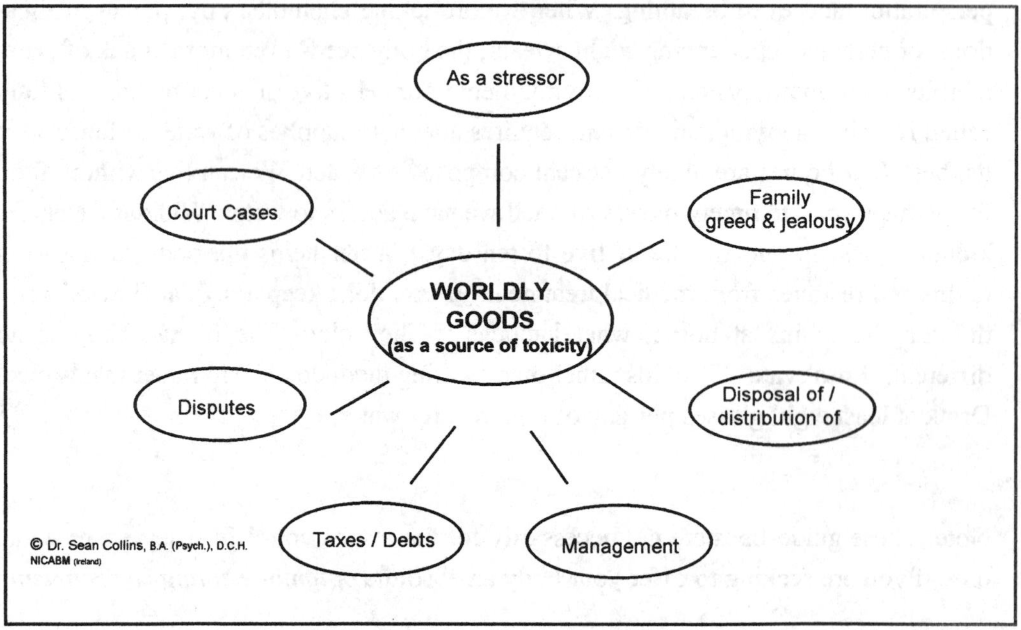

18. **Worldly Goods**: *Potential toxic factors for disposal... or to be* ***'put on hold'***

Vitamins and Minerals

A significant part of offering your body the best chance of healing is making sure your vitamin intake is adequate. How do you do this when you may be feeling generally unwell or undergoing treatment with side effects like nausea, vomiting etc.? The answer is by no means straightforward.

Medical knowledge about nutrition, and in particular about vitamins, remains incomplete, but certain trends are emerging. Patients are often caught in the middle. They hear of the usefulness of some vitamin or mineral for a certain condition, but then they ask for advice, their doctors often dismiss their questions. The vitamins we get from eating a varied diet are probably of better quality and do us more good than the synthetic variety. However, if you are unable to eat a very good diet, due to your illness, treatment or food intolerance, then it will do you no harm to take a multivitamin tablet. It is wise to check first with your doctor, though it is likely that he or she will advise a moderate amount of vitamins only.

Large doses of some vitamins can be harmful: vitamin A, for example, found in liver and several other fatty foods, is metabolised in the liver and can cause toxic effects if taken in excess. On the other hand, some vitamins in larger amounts have effects (largely ignored by many nutritionists and doctors) which may make them useful as treatments for particular problems. It is up to you to explore and find out what may be useful for you!

Vitamin C is a popular favourite to take as a supplement. It is needed by the body on a daily basis to aid tissue healing. It's role in the prevention of infections is still controversial, but given that it is harmless, even in large doses, if you want to take it, that's fine. Nobel prize winner, Dr. Linus Pauling claimed that 1-3 grams a day of Vitamin C can help to retard the progression of certain cancers and, in certain cases, to cause it to go into remission. Dr. Andrew Weil describes it as "useful as an antioxidant, cancer fighter, and immune system protector." The debate goes on.

There has also been some interesting research on the link between heart disease and vitamin E. A study of a large number of men in Scandinavia showed that those with ischaemic heart disease had significantly lower levels of Vitamin E in their blood than healthy men. Vitamin E is found in oily fish which is, of course, also known to help lower cholesterol levels. It would therefore seem sensible, if you have heart disease, to make sure that you eat oily fish such as salmon, tuna, herring, mackerel on a regular basis, and consider a supplement of vitamin E, if you dislike oily fish or if you want to make absolutely certain you have an adequate intake. Dr. Andrew Weil describes Vitamin E as a powerful and natural antioxidant offering protection against heart attacks and thrombotic strokes, which is essentially non-toxic-even in mega-doses. A recent study in England showed that 400 i.u. a day cut likelihood of repeat heart attack by 75%!

Mega-doses of most vitamins are automatically dumped by the body if not required. Minerals, on the other hand, are a complex subject and it is important to seek medical advice before considering mineral supplements. Be aware that many drugs, including diuretics, can alter the balance of minerals in the blood, and that some cancers may cause high levels of calcium in the blood, which can make you feel tired, nauseated and unwell.

Reduced levels of magnesium, zinc and other minerals are a rare cause of illness in the general population and unusual even in the presence of serious illness such as cancer. The body needs only tiny amounts of minerals, and usually manages to maintain levels adequately by its own feedback mechanisms. Calcium and mineral levels can be measured by a blood test if your doctor thinks it necessary.

Your Notes

Life Planning

Even for a short trip abroad, most people will prepare **a list** including where they are going, what they want to see or do and what they will need (passport, tickets, money, clothes etc.). The majority of people, however, wander through life, rarely if ever committing to paper what they really want, and **then** they wonder why they encounter **disappointment** , or become run-down or ill.

In 1953, a student in a university in the United States found that less than three per cent of his class had a written life plan. Twenty years later, a researcher checked with the class of '53 and found that the three per cent with written goals had accumulated **more wealth** than all of the other ninety-seven per cent together ! While only wealth was measured in that study, it was proof positive that the unconscious mind responds to clear direction!

Principles of Life Planning For Challenged People

If you have a 'life threatening' illness, it is likely that your unconscious mind received some sort of negative message when you were first diagnosed. Depression and negative thinking have been shown to suppress immune function in the body. If you want to enhance your immune function, carrying out a review of your life priorities and developing some precise long term plans for your future tends to let the unconscious mind know that you wish to be around to enjoy them!

The more precise and detailed your plans, the more effectively the unconscious mind will work towards achieving them. Life plans should be reviewed regularly (and, if necessary, changed) for about a month after the first completion. Clearly defined long term goals provide the basis for short term goals and action plans.

The Ten Most Wonderful Things in My Life Right NOW!

(or the 10 things I would most hate to lose!)

1. ______________________________

2. ______________________________

3. ______________________________

4. ______________________________

5. ______________________________

6. ______________________________

7. ______________________________

8. ______________________________

9. ______________________________

10. ______________________________

The Ten Least Wonderful Things in My Life Right NOW!

(or the 10 things I would just love to be rid of!)

1. ______________________________

2. ______________________________

3. ______________________________

4. ______________________________

5. ______________________________

6. ______________________________

7. ______________________________

8. ______________________________

9. ______________________________

10. ______________________________

NOW, on (**to-day's** date): ____________________

1. I am ____
   (Where are you in terms of career/occupation/job?)

2. I own ____
   (What do you own or possess that's meaningful to you)?

3. I am accomplishing ______________________________________
   (in terms of your personal development, life ambitions, hopes & dreams?)

4. I am living ____
   (location in the world?)

5. My net worth is: £ ______________

6. I earn annually: £ ______________

7. My spiritual development is ____
(Where are you, now, in terms of evolution of the spiritual or non-material side of yourself?)

8. My physical health is ____
(activity capability?)

9. My special relationships are____
(What are your special relationships? What sort of shape are they in?)

10. My hobbies are____
(What do you do just for plain fun or enjoyment?)

11. Contributing (to others) ____
(What do you do for others, in particular, for those who are not family or friends?)

Time ______________________________

Money______________________________

Other______________________________

In 20 Years at age _______ I imagine or picture myself as:

1. Being____
   (Where will you be in terms of career/occupation/job?)

2. Owning____
   (What will you own or possess that will be meaningful to you)?

3. Accomplishing ____
   (in terms of your personal development, life ambitions, hopes & dreams?)

4. Living__ ____
   (location in the world?)

5. Having net worth of: £ _______________

6. Earning annually: £ _______________

7. My spiritual development being______________________________________
(Where will you be in terms of evolution of the spiritual or non-material side of yourself?)

8. My physical health being ______________________________________
(activity capability?)

9. My special relationships being______________________________________
(What are your special relationships? What sort of shape are they in?)

10. My hobbies being____
(What will you do just for plain fun or enjoyment?)

11. Contributing (to others) ______________________________________
(What will you do for others, in particular, for those who are not family or friends?)

Time ______________________________

Money______________________________

Other ______________________________

In 10 Years, at age ______ I imagine or picture myself as:

1. Being____
   (Where will you be in terms of career/occupation/job?)

2. Owning____
   (What will you own or possess that will be meaningful to you)?

3. Accomplishing ____
   (in terms of your personal development, life ambitions, hopes & dreams?)

4. Living____
   (location in the world?)

5. Having net worth of: £ ________________

6. Earning annually: £ ________________

7. My spiritual development being____________________________________
(Where will you be in terms of evolution of the spiritual or non-material side of yourself?)

8. My physical health being _______________________________________
(activity capability?)

9. My special relationships being_____________________________________
(What are your special relationships? What sort of shape are they in?)

10. My hobbies being____
(What will you do just for plain fun or enjoyment?)

11. Contributing (to others) ____
(What will you do for others, in particular, for those who are not family or friends?)

Time ______________________________

Money______________________________

Other ______________________________

In 5 Years, at age _______ I imagine or picture myself as:

1. Being____
   (Where will you be in terms of career/occupation/job?)

2. Owning____
   (What will you own or possess that will be meaningful to you)?

3. Accomplishing ____
   (in terms of your personal development, life ambitions, hopes & dreams?)

4. Living____
   (location in the world?)

5. Having net worth of: £ ________________

6. Earning annually: £ ________________

7. My spiritual development being____

(Where will you be in terms of evolution of the spiritual or non-material side of yourself?)

8. My physical health being ____
(activity capability?)

9. My special relationships being____
(What are your special relationships? What sort of shape are they in?)

10. My hobbies being____
(What will you do just for plain fun or enjoyment?)

11. Contributing (to others) ____
(What will you do for others, in particular, for those who are not family or friends?)

Time ________________________________

Money________________________________

Other ________________________________

In 30 days, I imagine or picture myself as:

1. Being____
   (Where will you be in terms of career/occupation/job?)

2. Owning____
   (What will you own or possess that will be meaningful to you)?

3. Accomplishing __________________________________
   (in terms of your personal development, life ambitions, hopes & dreams?)

4. Living____
   (location in the world?)

5. Having net worth of: £ ________________

6. Earning annually: £ ________________

7. My spiritual development being_______________________________
(Where will you be in terms of evolution of the spiritual or non-material side of yourself?)

8. My physical health being _______________________________
(activity capability?)

9. My special relationships being_______________________________
(What are your special relationships? What sort of shape are they in?)

10. My hobbies being_______________________________
(What will you do just for plain fun or enjoyment?)

11. Contributing (to others) _______________________________
(What will you do for others, in particular, for those who are not family or friends?)

Time _______________________

Money_______________________

Other _______________________

Action Plan

What are the ten most effective things I can do, during the next thirty days, to get me on my way towards my life plan?

1. ______________________________

2. ______________________________

3. ______________________________

4. ______________________________

5. ______________________________

6. ______________________________

7. ______________________________

8. ______________________________

9. ______________________________

10. ______________________________

Laughter

"A merry heart does good like a medicine, but a broken spirit dries the bones"

(Proverbs 17:22)

Norman Cousins, former editor of the *Saturday Review,* brought the attention of the medical community to the possibility that laughter may have a healing potential. In 1964, he was diagnosed with ankylosing spondylitis, a progressive degenerative disease of the collagen tissue. His physicians gave him little hope for recovery, indicating that a possible cause of his illness was heavy-metal poisoning. From reading Hans Selye's book: *The stress of life* (1956), Cousins recalled that research showed that *negative* emotions (such as anger sadness, fear, hurt, guilt, depression etc) could create chemical changes in the body that could lead to eventual adrenal exhaustion. He suspected that *positive* emotions (such as faith, hope, confidence and joy) might create changes in the body which would enhance his recovery process.

Since the behaviour of laughter tends to open a person to these positive emotions, Cousins began viewing funny films to stimulate laughter (belly laughs). After each laughing episode, he noted he could sleep more comfortably without the need for analgesia or sedation. He also discovered that laughter stimulated a decrease in his sedimentation rate, indicating a reversal of the inflammatory response. After his recovery, Cousins was appointed an adjunct professor at UCLA Medical School where he lead research into the beneficial effects of laughter.

Clinical research is now demonstrating clearly that humour and laughter in our lives can significantly enhance the effectiveness of the immune system. Illness, either acute onset or chronic is generally a stressful event. Hospitalisation, separation from family, invasive procedures, complex technology or unfamiliar caregivers, all can create feelings of anxiety, loneliness, discomfort, anger, panic and depression for patients. These emotions are now known to produce physiological changes that interfere with the body's natural 'fight back' mechanisms at the precise time when these need to be boosted. Humour and laughter can reverse this.

Humour is a perceptual process which is processed in the mind whereas laughter is a behavioural response, it happens in the body!

Interesting Thought on Laughter

Laughter has been proven to provide a counterbalance to *stress*
Laughter has been proven to provide a counterbalance to *helplessness*
Laughter has been proven to provide a counterbalance to *depression*
In the face of serious illness, laughter is sometimes hard to start but only at first.
Laughter creates biochemical changes in the body which help the body
Caregivers need to laugh also

Clinical research shows that technically laughter causes ....

Serum cortisol to drop (enhances immune response)
The baseline of adrenalin to lower (enhances immune response)
Increases natural killer (NK) cell numbers and activity (NK cells attack cancer cells)
Increases numbers of helper-T cells (better immune function)
Higher salivary immunoglobulin A (IgA) our first line defence against infections.

Possible Interventions

Funny Videos
Funny Films
Actively seeking out positive good humoured and funny people
Looking for things to laugh at in everyday life
Avoiding negative people
Giving yourself permission to laugh

Cousins, N. (1979) Anatomy of an Illness, New York, Norton & Co.
Cousins, N. (1989) Head First,- The Biology of Hope, New York, Dutton.

The 'Swish' Pattern

Developed by Dr Richard Bandler and Dr John Grinder back in the 1970's, the swish pattern is used for changing any habitual way of thinking or behaving. If certain situations tend to trigger you into unresourceful mental states or behaviours you don't want, then this is simple yet highly effective tool. Swish patterns are triggers or anchors which create automatic unconscious momentum towards a compelling future. You install new choices for reacting rather than change or remove old habits.

Process

Step 1. In your mind, create a picture or image of a habit, a behaviour, a pattern or situation which you want to change (perhaps where you are stuck!)
This is picture **No. 1**.

Step 2. Now, in your mind, create a **disassociated** image of: how you wish to behave or react differently, or ... the person you wish to become, or ... the outcome you want i.e. tumour to shrink, or wound to heal... (**vividly and in detail**). This is picture **No. 2**.

Step 3. Now, in your mind, put up the image **No. 1** and in the lower right hand corner of this image, place a **small** dark version of picture **No. 2**.

Step 4. Now, *very quickly*, shrink image **No. 1** down while at **the same time**, have image **No. 2** become large, bright and attractive and then, immediately let the images go and open your eyes. Speed is of the essence. Make sure the old image fades at exactly the same time as the new one explodes onto the stage of your inner mind. It can help this technique if you accompany the switch by an internal or external 'Swishhhhhhh' sound. You must see and feel that small dark picture (**No. 2**) suddenly become huge and bright and explode through the first picture (**No. 1**), destroying it and replacing it.

Step 5. Repeat the process a minimum of five times with each project and enjoy the results.

The Four Stages of Learning

Fighting back against serious illness often involves learning new skills. Unfortunately, this tends to be at the very time when you are feeling perhaps worried, frightened, angry or impatient. I find, therefore, that health-challenged clients are loath to engage with enthusiasm in acquiring new abilities.

Whenever you find yourself 'stuck' and unable to move forward, beating yourself up or berating your performance will only make things worse. Regardless of the context, it is useful to return to the 'Conscious Incompetence' stage, purposefully, allowing yourself to 'flounder about' and re-learn what you need to learn.

Stage 1: **Unconscious Incompetence,** is when you are unable to perform some task or activity but you can't think of any reason why you'd want to.

Stage 2: **Conscious Incompetence,** is when you now become aware of a need to be able to perform some task or activity, yet when you try it, your performance is poor or disappointing (Many people use this phase to focus on their supposed lack of ability, and sometimes even try to skip this phase altogether! Few give themselves permission to recognise this as an **essential** stage in achieving excellence in anything.)

Stage 3: **Conscious Competence,** is when a person, through training and practice, is able to perform the required task or activity. However they have to retain a lot of conscious and 'self-conscious' involvement in the activity, thereby performing below their optimum capability.

Stage 4: **Unconscious Competence.** Excellence comes when, having practised and corrected, you are able to relinquish conscious involvement in a process and just get on with doing the job excellently.

Reference: Joseph O Connor & John Seymour (1990 [9]), *Introducing NLP.*

Part 3

An Actual Programme

(Ten weeks to tip the balance)

Tipping the scales

A 10 Weeks programme for those who want to fight back and to heal.

The following is a ten-week programme in behavioural change. To use an old cliché "If you keep doing what you've always done, you'll keep getting what you always got. If you want **something different**, then you'll have to do something different".

So having read through different ideas and techniques, if you're reading here, you've probably decided to attempt 'something different'.

This programme is designed to help people, both patients and carers, to mobilise their inner psychological resources for taking better care of themselves as a complement to the medical treatment they receive. The objective is to identify, and then provide an 'optimum' environment in each of the following life areas: physical, psychological, emotional and spiritual. Insofar as is possible, it is based on 'evidence' from research in the fields of behavioural medicine and psychoneuroimmunology.

Although each week has a specific theme or themes, each builds on the work of the previous one. Research has shown that there is a definite 'dose' effect in these type of approaches. In other words, the more you do, the more you get, the less you do the less you get; it's up to you! Like a menu in a restaurant, the programme seeks to offer **choices and options**. Even if you can engage in only half of the techniques or can only give a 50% commitment, **this is fine** too!

Numerous studies suggest that more than 85% of participants will produce clinically measurable improvements. You can too. Do remember, if you start this programme, you are committing to an immediate lifestyle change by practising for one to two hours a day (this is generally a pleasant and restful experience).

Steps to Fighting Back

- Understand your diagnosis
- Feel and experience what you're feeling
- Get a second opinion
- Get a counsellor/mentor/strategist
- Decide and specify exactly what you want to achieve
- Go for the best anyone has ever achieved before
- Explore all possible cause components in your illness
- Explore all possible solution components for your 'fight-back' plan
- Settle on a specific plan and a time-scale
- Explore, and have solutions for, the inevitable pitfalls along your chosen path
- Settle on an evidence procedure for success/failure. How will you know you've succeeded?
- Contract with yourself to follow your plan for a set period and then review
- Take action, notice what's working and what's not working, Change your approach
- Keep changing your approach until you get what you want

Week 1

Get an independent second opinion ASAP if you have **any** doubts

Start meditation

Decide on what to eat & drink, when and how and start mindful eating (optimum)

Select a coach/mentor/counsellor

Develop a well-formed outcome for yourself

Week 2

Start yoga and find a class/teacher

Start visualisation

Continue daily meditation
Continue daily mindful eating (optimum)

Week 3

Review diet and consider vitamin/mineral supplementation

Start self-hypnosis & visualisation

Start 1:4:2 breath training

Start massage/healing therapy

Continue daily meditation
Continue daily yoga
Continue daily mindful eating (optimum)

Week 4

Develop a 20 year life plan and review this daily for the week

Continue daily meditation
Continue daily yoga
Continue daily self-hypnosis and visualisation
Continue daily 1:4:2 breathing
Continue daily mindful eating (optimum)

Week 5

Start laughter therapy

Start Qi Gong

Start challenging limiting beliefs

Explore secondary gain

Continue daily meditation
Continue daily yoga
Continue daily 1:4:2 breathing
Continue daily self-hypnosis
Continue daily visualisation
Continue daily mindful eating (optimum)

Week 6

Explore releasing emotional baggage with journalling for the week (Pennebaker process)

Use Time Line Therapy or other psychological intervention for negative emotion release

Carry out a review with your mentor of all possible causes and solutions

Continue seeking laughter & non-competitive play opportunities
Continue daily meditation
Continue daily yoga
Continue daily 1:4:2 breathing
Continue daily self-hypnosis & visualisation
Continue daily mindful eating (optimum)

Week 7

Review 'deep dark secrets'

Review your use of resources: time, energy, relationships, confidence etc

Continue seeking laughter & non-competitive play opportunities
Continue daily meditation
Continue daily yoga
Continue daily 1:4:2 breathing
Continue daily self-hypnosis
Continue daily visualisation
Continue daily mindful eating (optimum)

Week 8

Again explore releasing emotional baggage with journalling for the week (Pennebaker process)

Continue seeking laughter & non-competitive play opportunities
Continue daily meditation
Continue daily yoga
Continue daily 1:4:2 breathing
Continue daily self-hypnosis
Continue daily visualisation
Continue daily mindful eating (optimum)

Week 9

Continue seeking laughter & non-competitive play opportunities
Continue daily meditation
Continue daily yoga
Continue daily 1:4:2 breathing
Continue daily self-hypnosis
Continue daily visualisation
Continue daily mindful eating (optimum)

Week 10

Again, explore releasing emotional baggage with journalling for the week (Pennebaker process)

Review your 20 year life plan

Continue seeking laughter & non-competitive play opportunities
Continue daily meditation
Continue daily yoga
Continue daily 1:4:2 breathing
Continue daily self-hypnosis
Continue daily visualisation
Continue daily mindful eating (optimum)

Week 11

Review the extent to which you have achieved your outcome?

Part 4

Appendices

Eight-week Behavioural Change Research Programme

(**1996** Pilot Study Proposal)

Programme Objective: To explore the clinical effectiveness of self-regulatory behavioural strategies in enhancing health, and as a complement to mainstream medical care in coping with common life challenges.

Programme Background: In 1990, the medical journal, the Lancet, reported the results of the behavioural change programme, developed by Dr. Dean Ornish, which proved that the progress of heart disease and, in particular, clogged arteries, could be reversed by behavioural change. Two years previously, Dr David Spiegel, at Stanford, demonstrated that the life expectancy of Stage-4 breast cancer patients could be doubled, using a particular form of weekly group work. In 1991, the Institute of Psychiatry, University of London, released the results of a 13 year study, carried out by psychiatrist H.J. Eysenck and R. Grossarth-Maticek, which showed that a particular form of therapy/psychological intervention could reduce the risk of premature death by a significant 75% among 'Type C' (cancer prone) people.

This research programme will concentrate on using a synthesis of the above programmes to seek to manage pain, reduce high blood pressure, and reduce elevated cholesterol, and positively affect other life challenging conditions through behavioural change. No drugs are used.

Project Leaders:
Medical/Behavioural: Dr. Anthony Sharkey, M.B., B.C.H, BAO, D.C.H. (01-660 9332)
Psychological/Behavioural: Dr. Sean Collins, B.A (Psych.), D.C.H. (Psychotherapist) (01-283 1000)

Duration: Eight Wednesday mornings, commencing Wednesday, 2nd October, 1996

Fees: None

Venue: St Michael's Hospital, Dun Laoghaire. (The Large Meeting Room)

Time: 10.00 a.m. - 12.30 p.m.

Medical Supervision: Whilst participants are medically monitored in the course of the programme, it is suggested that they advise their General Practitioner of their participation in the programme.

Commitment: Although a participant is free to withdraw from the programme or any aspect of it, or may be asked to withdraw on medical grounds, potential participants are requested to give serious consideration to committing to completing the entire programme.

Home work: Typically requiring 45-60 minutes of home project work per day

Support: Participants are free to bring a spouse or friend who will not be monitored, but will be expected to participate fully for the complete programme.

Course Components

1. **Psychological Testing** using a protocol devised by Dr. Hans Selye, founder of the Canadian Institute of Stress, and considered to be the father of modern stress research.

2. **Biological Ageing** using the Morgan Biological ageing protocol, developed by Dr. Robert Morgan.

3. **Journalling** based on the work of Dr. James Pennebaker, professor of psychology at SMU, Dallas, Texas, USA, whose work has shown that immune function can be raised, and health significantly improved by journalling life traumas.

4. **Yoga,** based on the work of Dr. Dean Ornish (who proved that the progress of heart disease and, in particular, clogged arteries, could be reversed), on the work of Jon Kabat-Zinn at the University of Massachusetts Medical Centre, and various other authors.

5. **Meditation** based on the work of Jon Kabat-Zinn, Harvard Cardiologist, Dr. Herbert Benson, and also the TM technique.

6. **Visualisation,** based on the work of Dr. Carl Simonton, MD, author of "Getting Well Again", and Deirdre Davis Brigham, author of "Imagery for Getting Well" and director of the 'Getting Well' programme in Florida, one of the most highly regarded programmes in behavioural medicine in the world.

7. **Breath Training** based on standard yoga breath training, and the work of Lymphologist, Dr Jack Shields, in stimulating immune function.

8. **Self-Hypnosis** based on the work of Professor David Spiegel at Stanford, who demonstrated that the life expectancy of Stage-4 breast-cancer patients could be doubled, using a particular form of group work along with self-hypnosis.

9. **Time-line Therapy,** developed by Dr. Tad James, which is used for effortlessly releasing old negative emotions, such as anger, sadness, fear, hurt, guilt and resentment, **without** having to access the original causative events.

10. **Diet & Eating**, which will explore optimum ways to feed the body.

11. **Life Planning/Life Purpose**, which will explore clarity in life direction and communicate this to the unconscious, so as to positively affect health.

12. **Language and Health,** based on the work of several authors, exploring how language can impact both positively or negatively on health.

Measurements

The following measurements will be taken at the beginning **and** end of the programme:

1. Weight	2. Blood pressure	3. Body Fat
4. Heart Rate	5. Cholesterol	6. Selye Stress personality
7. Biological Age		

'Fighting Back'

'The St. Michael's Project'
(A research project using behavioural change in fighting back against critical illness)

Oct. - Nov., 1996

Dr. Sean Collins, B.A. (Psych.), D.C.H.
Ardagh Clinic
32 Dawson Street, Dublin 2

Tel: (01) 260 0118 or (01) 283 1000

Lord grant me the courage to change what can be changed ,
the serenity to accept what cannot be changed,
and the wisdom to know one from the other

Reinhold Niebhur (theologian)

Acknowledgements

The Participants
Valerie Collins
Rhoda Draper
Marlene ffrench Mullen
Dr Anthony Sharkey (Ratnabandhu)
Sanghapala
Susanne Barry
Sister Columba, Matron, St Michael's Hospital
Medical Lab. at the Meath Hospital
Participant supporters

Contents

Background & Definitions

The Society of Behavioural Medicine defines Behavioural Medicine as "The interdisciplinary field concerned with the development and integration of behavioural and biomedical science and techniques relevant to the understanding of health and illness, and the application of this knowledge and these techniques to prevention, diagnosis, treatment and rehabilitation". They describe their mission as seeking to "foster the development and application of knowledge on the relationship among health, illness and behaviour".

The Stanford University Department of Psychiatry and Behavioural Sciences states in it's mission statement: "Physical, environmental and psychosocial stressors exert a profound influence on neuro-endocrine-immune functioning..... The body does not differentiate carefully between different types of stressors during a stress response..... The disease itself is a stressor, as are the treatment and subsequent psychosocial changes. These stressors may lead to detrimental changes within the body, which can be minimised through psychosocial intervention .... These benefits (from such interventions) may lead, in turn, to delayed disease progression and prolonged survival time, as well as improvement in quality of life"

The motivation to carry out this study came from my own clinical experience as a psychotherapist working with clients facing life threatening illnesses. Clients diagnosed with cancer or heart disease would frequently report that when they asked their doctor "What else can I do?", they would be told "Nothing..... just take the tablets, chemotherapy, radiotherapy etc." For a majority of people, this response tends to engender a sense of personal powerlessness, which research suggests actually interferes with, or lowers, immune function. At the very time when people need their immune function enhanced, often the diagnosis and/or medical attitude lowers it further.

This research programme was about exploring methods, which are **evidence based,** or which have been the subject of reasonable scientific scrutiny. The goal was to offer an optimum setting, or healing environment, to trigger the body's normal self-healing mechanisms. This pilot study was intended to determine if the clinical results being achieved abroad were possible in an Irish context.

General Information

Title: Behavioural Change Research Programme - Pilot Study

Author: Dr Sean Collins, B.A (Psych), D.C.H. (Psychotherapist).

Objective: To explore the clinical effectiveness of self-regulatory behavioural strategies in enhancing health and as a complement to mainstream medical care in dealing with common health crises.

Project Leaders: Medical/Behavioural: Dr. Anthony Sharkey, M.B., B.C.H., BAO, D.C.H.
Psychological/Behavioural: Dr. Sean Collins, B.A.(Psych.), D.C.H.

Study Period: Wednesday 2nd October 1996 - Wednesday, 27th November 1996 (8 weeks).

Protocols Utilised: Modified Morgan's Ageing Scale (by Dr. Robert Morgan)
Modified Vitality Factor (By Dr Richard Earle)
'Fighting Back' Programme - Vsn. 1 (Dr Sean Collins)

Number of Participants: 21 (8 male, 13 female)

Average Age: 51

Presenting Conditions: Various (see Appendix 2)

Source of Participants: Advertisement for volunteers in the national press

Preconditions for Admission: To be included, participants had to be facing some significant life-threatening or quality of life threatening condition, and be willing to commit to eight Wednesday mornings (10.00-12.30), along with approximately one hour's homework per day. 28 were accepted as volunteers, 24 commenced the programme and 21 completed.

Compliance: In order to explore the 'self-regulatory' aspect of the programme, no formal reporting on compliance with the protocol was required from participants.

Venue: St Michael's Hospital, Dunlaoghaire, Co. Dublin.
(Please note that this was an independent study and neither the management nor the medical staff of St. Michael's Hospital were involved in the design or administration of this study, although grateful thanks are extended for their co-operation and the use of their facilities.)

Project Staff: 7

Funding: Dr Sean Collins, B.A. (Psych.), D.C.H.

Summary of Findings (Abstract)

1. Ageing

Average Chronological Age: 51.4 years
Group Average Biological Age at commencement: 48.7 years
Group Average Biological Age on completion: 43.3 years (11.1% reduction in biological age)
(Note: 85% of participants moved in the predicted direction.)

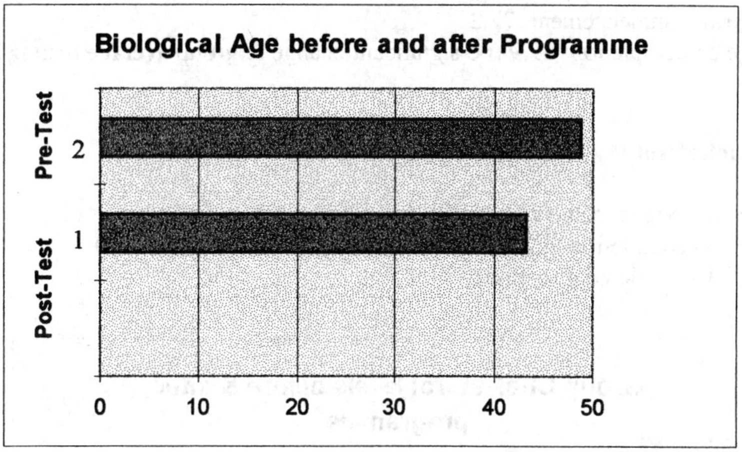

2. Blood Pressure (Systolic)

Group Average at commencement: 147 Group Average on completion: 129 (9.8% reduction in systolic blood pressure) (Note: 78% of participants moved in the predicted direction).

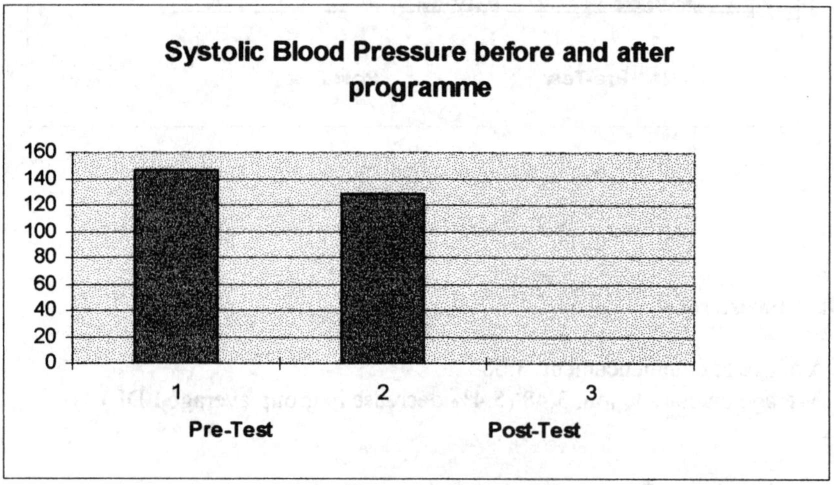

3. Blood Pressure (Diastolic)

Group Average at commencement: 96.4
Group Average on completion: 87.8 (8.8% reduction in diastolic blood pressure)
(83% of participants moved in the predicted direction)

4. Resting Heart Rate

Group Average at commencement: 72.2
Group Average on completion: 69.9 (no significant change in group average resting heart rate)

5. Overall Cholesterol

Group Average at commencement: 6.56
Group Average on completion: 6.21 (5.3% reduction in overall cholesterol)
(87% moved in the predicted direction)

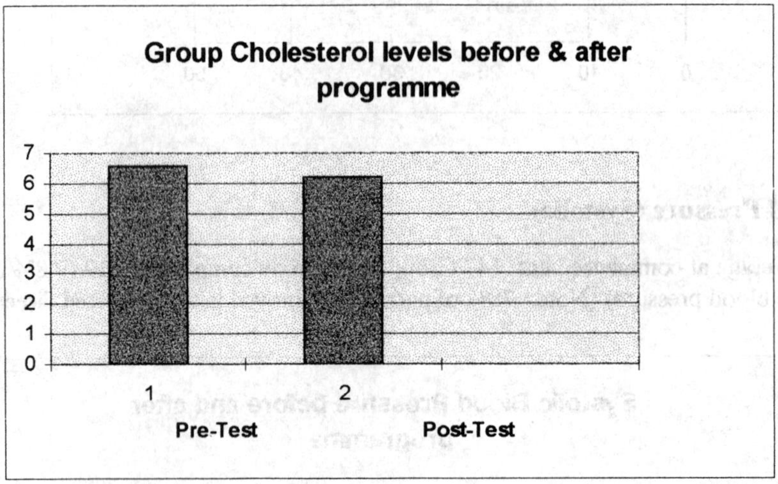

6. LDL Cholesterol

Group Average at commencement: 3.68
Group Average on completion: 3.48 (5.4% decrease in group average LDL)

7. Psychological Well Being (Vitality Factor)

Group Average at commencement: 356
Group Average on completion: 399
Group average VF improved by 15%
(note an increase in Vitality factor means an improvement)

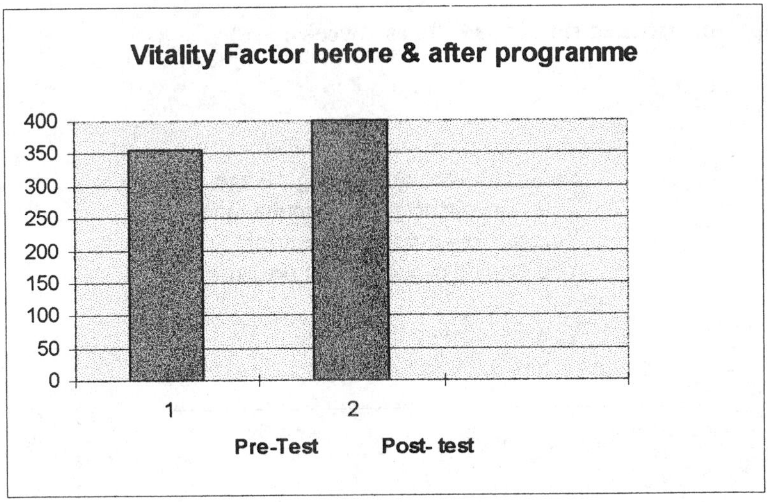

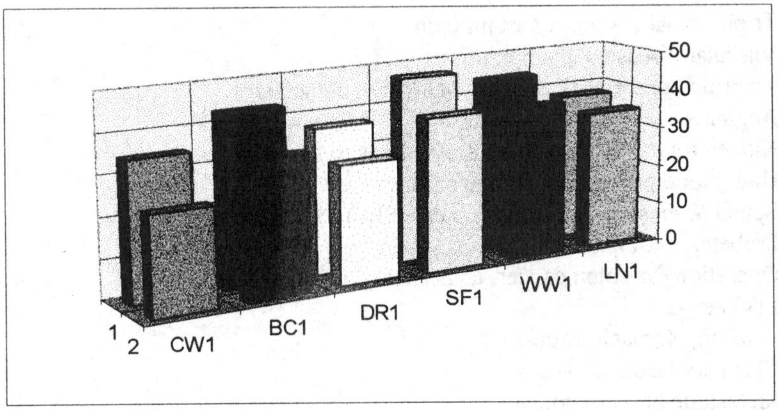

Stress-personality profiles, before and after programme

Note: The Vitality Factor (VF) is a modified version of the stress inventory used in a comparable Canadian Study carried out by the Canadian Institute of Stress. It measures 'stress fitness', the combination of inherited resources, life style habits, and learned skills that help or hinder the ability to cope with stressors of whatever intensity. It offers a very good indication of rate of ageing and stressotype profile.

Conclusions

This group demonstrated that in as little as 7 weeks:

You can lower your biological age
You can enhance your immune function
You can lower your cholesterol
You can lower your blood pressure
and
You can change the odds

Presenting Problems

Heart disease
Chronic brucellosis
Triple spinal fusion - constant pain
Vascular disease, leg amputation
Arthritic knee + back & groin pain, high cholesterol
Angina
Kidney reflux, fibromyalgia, nerve damage
High blood pressure & stomach ulcer
Spinal & muscle dislocation - pain, + Irritable bowel syndrome
Diabetes, orthopaedic problems - pain
Operation for colon cancer, angioplasty, tinnitus, tension
Leukaemia
Tension, stomach trouble
Coronary heart disease
Metastatic brain tumour
Irritable bowel syndrome
Lupus

Canadian Study

Published mid '80's by the Canadian Institute of Stress

Number of Applicants: 1,828

Number of Participants: 623

Criteria for Selection:

Had to be manifesting the range of symptoms characterising the 5 stages of distress. Anyone currently in medical treatment for any chronic physical disorder or in psychotherapy or on continuing medication was excluded.

Ageing:

Average Chronological Age on entry: 36.4 years
Group Average Biological Age at commencement: 42.1 years
Group Average Biological Age at 4 months: 39.7 years (5.7% reduction in biological age)
Group Average Biological Age at 8 months: 33.9 years (19.5% reduction in biological age)
Note: 80% of participants moved in the predicted direction.)

Other Interesting Results

	4 months	8 months
Immunoglobulin A increase	24%	31%
T cells increase	16%	28%
Oxygen uptake increase	32%	47%
Body fat decrease	22%	36%

Study of Clinical Application of Behavioural Medicine with Life Threatening and Chronic Quality of Life Threatening Conditions

Outline Proposal for 1998 Study

Introduction: Studies in recent years by Spiegel *et al.* (1989) and Fawzy *et al.* (1990) suggest that psychosocial and behavioural intervention can positively influence outcomes for patients suffering with life threatening diseases such as cancer and heart disease, both in terms of life expectancy and quality of life. An Irish pilot study carried out in 1996 showed promising results in clinical biological and psychological measures.

Objective:
1. To demonstrate that patients can participate effectively in the management of critical and chronic conditions and produce measurable results and
2. To develop an effective 'results based' protocol which can be taught to medical personnel, psychologists and counsellors who regularly interact with such challenged people.

Proposal: To carry out a prospective randomised controlled study from a self-selecting (in terms of wishing to 'fight back') population to determine whether a specific protocol of guided self-regulatory behavioural/psychological interventions, as a complement to standard medical care, can produce measurable and sustainable change over a three month period.

The Protocol: This will comprise various previously tested elements from the fields of behavioural and health psychology (see appendix).

Participants: These will be volunteers suffering with life threatening conditions such as cancer, aids or heart disease and also quality of life threatening conditions such as arthritis, asthma, diabetes and systemic lupus. (If you wish to volunteer, an application form is included in the following pages)

Numbers: 80-100 to be selected from a volunteer group who will be sourced via newspaper advertising and radio/TV programmes. 50% of participants will be assigned to an intervention group and the balance to a control group. For ethical reasons, the control group will be offered the option of undergoing a similar programme six months after completion of the study.

Duration: Recruitment take place in November and December 1997. The programme will run for ten weeks and will commence, in mid-January with a three-day saturation training session where patients will become familiar with the individual components of the programme. This be followed by ten weekly half-day sessions. Limited follow up will be carried out at three and six months following completion of the programme,

Supervision: It is proposed that the design and administration of the project and testing will be subjected to rigorous academic and medical supervision

Measures: Participants will be assessed at the beginning and end of the programme for certain physical measures, possibly including: resting heart rate, blood pressure, body fat, lipid profiles, Immunolglobulin A, Biological ageing (Morgan Scale). Psychological assessment may include depression scales, perception of control scales, optimism scales etc.

Outline Protocol Components

Yoga (IYA)/Progressive Exercise
Meditation (Benson)
Self-hypnosis (Spiegel)
Visualisation (Brigham)
Breath Work (1:3:2)
Mayr Eating/dietary counselling
Life-Planning
Cognitive Restructuring/Reframing/Rule of 6
Time Line Emotion Release Therapy (Dr T. James)
Counselling (non-directive)
Laughter (Cousins)
Journalling (Pennebaker)
Group Work/Buddying (Spiegel)
Taped Relaxation Sessions (changed weekly)
Immune Power Personality Review (traits & habits)
Secondary Gain Review

Study of Clinical Application of Behavioural Medicine with Life Threatening and Chronic Quality of Life Threatening Conditions

Volunteer General Information Sheet

Participants must:

a) Have been diagnosed with a life threatening condition such as cancer, heart disease, (but be deemed to be likely to survive at least one year).
   or

b) Have been diagnosed with some significant 'quality of life' threatening condition such as arthritis, asthma, rheumatoid arthritis, multiple sclerosis, etc.

c) Be currently under medical supervision

d) May not be involved in any similar structured 'fight back' programme

e) Be no younger than 21 and no older than 75

f) Be willing to commit to at least one hour a day of personal work at home during the ten weeks of the programme

g) Be willing to attend at an intensive three-day group training session at the commencement of the project

h) Be willing to attend a weekly half-day session in Dublin, from 9.30 a.m. - 1.00 p.m., for ten sequential Fridays

i) Be willing to attend a personal counselling session at least once every 2 week during the protocol

j) Be willing to be filmed as part of the project and possibly interviewed for a subsequent documentary

k) Be willing to undergo a blood test at the beginning and end of the project and also blood pressure, cholesterol, body fat (calliper test) and various psychological tests

l) No personal information will be disclosed. All personal information is kept confidential. All volunteer records will be under confidential control numbers.

m) Participants will be selected randomly from volunteers. One hundred people will be randomly selected who will all receive psychological and physical testing. Then, fifty of these will be assigned to a 'control' group and fifty to an 'intervention' group.

n) Where possible, volunteers will be invited to have a spouse, sibling or 'important other' to go through the ten week protocol. These people will be expected to participate alongside the volunteers and to do exactly what they do.

o) Volunteers in the 'intervention' group will go through the 10 week protocol whereas those in the 'control' group will be assessed and sent on their way. They will be required to return for testing at the end of the 10 weeks. When the results are published at the end of April, the members of the 'control' group will be invited to participate in the same protocol.

p) Those who volunteer, but who are not selected for either the control group or intervention group, will receive a monthly newsletter with detailed and specific information on the research project, which will be helpful to them in developing their own effective programmes.

q) No fees will be paid or requested.

1998 Behavioural Medicine Research Programme

Volunteer Application Sheet

(Block Capitals Please)

Name: ______________________________

Address: ______________________________

____

Tel (home): ______________ **Work**: ______________

Age: ______________

Sex: ______________

Medical Condition(s): ______________________________

____

Approximate Date(s) of Diagnosis: ______________

Medication(s): ______________________________

____

Name of GP: ______________________________

Address of GP: ______________________________

____

Tel No of GP: ______________

I understand that in volunteering, is possible that:

a) I may be assessed as unlikely to benefit from the programme,

or

b) I may not be selected due to volunteer numbers,

or

c) may be assigned to a 'control' or comparison group. I hereby authorise you to advise my doctor of my potential participation in the programme and if necessary to seek his advice.

Signed ______________________________ Date: ______________

The Future

This pilot study successfully replicated the type of results being achieved abroad. In the first quarter of 1998, the author plans to carry out a controlled, randomised, study of 100 similarly challenged individuals. This study will be subject to *rigorous* medical and academic scrutiny.

In recent years, there has been an explosion of interest in alternative and complementary medicine. However, few of these therapies have been subjected to scientific evaluation.

The objective of this 'controlled' study will be to produce an 'evidence based' protocol for use by individuals faced with a health crisis. It will also be used in the development of an effective training programme in behavioural medicine for therapists and medical personnel.

This study is scheduled to commence in January, 1998.

Exploring Alternative and Complementary Therapies

The following is a listing of points for consideration by anyone facing a life threatening or 'quality of life' threatening condition. This emerged from the reading of over 500 books in the area and more than 2,000 research papers. Potential sources of stress are listed, as well as sources of healing - these are sometimes interchangeable!

Having completed the ten-week basic programme, you are, here provided with an immediate check-list with which to brain-storm other areas for potential investigation with your 'important other' or health crisis counsellor. Many of the therapies listed here are untried and controversial so it is important to consider the following questions when considering any 'alternative' or complementary therapy:

1. Has research been done on this therapy? Is there evidence that it works?
2. Does it hurt?
3. What are the side effects?
4. Do I know anyone who has used it?
5. What did they think about it?
6. What would my doctor think?
7. How is it generally viewed by the medical profession?
8. Could it interfere with my current treatment?
9. Can I trust the practitioner?
10. What books have been written on it?.
11. How is it rated by guides to complementary therapies such as 'Health Which'?
12. Is there a national organisation of practitioners?
13. Is the practitioner you are considering a member in good standing of a national organisation?
14. Is the practitioner insured?
15. What will it cost?
16. What is the time commitment (for therapy sessions and for my own daily practice)?

The following is a check-list only. Specific descriptions of therapies can be found in reference books in libraries or from national organisations representing practitioners.

Established practitioners in any field are likely to be members of a national organisation and should be happy to provide you with their name and contact number. These organisations can sometimes be found in the Golden Pages.

Broad areas of potential intervention in a health crisis

Behavioural	Biological	Dietary	Environmental
Financial	Genetic	Medical	Complementary
Pharmacological	Physiological	Psychological	Emotional
Social/Sociological	Solo v Group	Spiritual/Religious	

365 Stressors, Therapies & Approaches

Abusive history (physical, sexual and/or emotional) resolution of .....
Acupressure
Acupuncture (needle)
Acupuncture (electro)
Acupuncture (laser)
Addictions (release - behaviours, reactions, substances etc)
Affiliations (sense of brotherhood or belonging)
Affirmations/praise (by self and others)
Aggression (dealing with)
Ageing (sense of)
Agitation/restlessness management
Allergies (kinesiology, Vega testing, conventional)
Alexander technique
Alternative & complementary treatments - discussing these with your doctor?
Alzheimer's disease (nursing of a patient)
Amino acid therapy
Anxiety/panic attacks management
Aromatherapy
Art therapy (as a form of expression)
Assertiveness training
Attitude (passive/assertive)
Autogenic training
Awareness/consciousness/living in 'NOW' (not in 'past/future' obsession)
Ayurvedic medicine
Bach flower remedies/essences
Balance in life (business/home/personal etc)
Baths & float tanks
Behaviours - damaging/healing/empowering
Behavioural change (knowledge v capabilities)
Beliefs-useful/unuseful,empowering/disempowering
Bereavement (see letting-go/grieving)
Bio-energetics
Biofeedback

Biological v chronological age
Blame/self-blame
Blood pressure management (as a biofeedback device)
Body (belief in the self-healing capability?)
Body image
Books/reading (balance - not all technical!)
Boredom management v new interests
Breath training: Pranayama, 1:4:2 lymph breathing
Bristol Clinic-type programmes (knowledge of/ interest in/ attitude towards)
Cholesterol management (as a biofeedback device)
Cancer (How I say it: 'I have cancer' (permanent), 'My body is cancering' (temporary)
Career (what stage am I at?)
Career (entrapment in)
Career (fears for continuance of)
Career (complete change of?)
Career (letting go) - "if I'm not 'x', who am I?"
Carers (rights of, and training course for), (abuse and manipulation of or by carers)
Carers (caring for yours)
Caring for others (as a form of healing?)
Cause v effect assessment (are you in charge in your life or are you like a leaf?)
Ceremony/ritual: stepping free of the mundane and the everyday
Chanting
Chelation (oral)
Chelation - EDTA (highly controversial!)
Childcraft (help with, communication with etc)
Childhood and upbringing (highs, lows and emotional baggage from)
Chiropractic (balance and alignment)
Chiropody (for feeling well)
Cholesterol management (as a biofeedback device)
Coach or health crisis counsellor (to help you develop and stay with a programme) (forging an alliance with and contracting with)
Colon appreciation & management
Colonic irrigation
Colour therapy
Competition/competitiveness management (self/others)
Communication with your medical doctor
Communication with employers, banks, health insurers etc.
Communication with yourself (your inner dialogue)
Communication with others (general, and regarding your illness)
Community (your place in; your relationship with; your sense of..)
Compulsions (your deep, dark secrets)
Concentration and focus (problems with)
Conflict (ability to engage in, and find resolution - re-solution)
Control of illness (your sense of - at which stage of the illness are you?)
Concerned, committed enthusiastic medics (evaluation of)
Conflicts (dealing with)
Congruence (Are you walking your talk?)
Consistency (Are you staying on track?)
Constipation, toxic (food passage time)
Control (sense of) in terms of : career? family? personal? internal? external?
Contribution (sense of)
Coping skills training

Cost of care: Fears about money? Fears about being hospitalised? Fear of losing control?

Counselling: Telling others? Telling kids? Telling self at a deep level?

Cranio-sacral therapy

Criticism (dealing with)

Crying/tears (role and frequency - not only OK, it's potentially essential!)

Crystal healing

Dance & movement (as a form of expression)

Death - Its OK to die (guilt issues around this)

Death - planning for ... avoiding disputes, wills etc.

Death (mentally preparing for yours - "what's it like to be not here?")

Death (God and Judgement!)

Death wish (Do you have one?)

Deceit (self/others)

Deep dark secrets (repressed - gay, criminal, inadequacy, sexual problems, perversions. etc)

Denial ("it can't be true ... it's not true..")

Depression management (high grade/low grade/clinical). Help is essential!

Despair management: "Doctor says there's no point in doing anything more", "What else can I do?"

Detoxification (Mayr etc.)

Diagnosis (accepting/denying/getting second opinions)

Diet - macrobiotic, vegetarian, vegan, Cancer Society etc.

Diet and nutrition - food combining, fats, sugars, food volume reduction, alcohol, caffeine, salt, fibre, cholesterol

Dignity/vanity (personal entitlement to)

Disease ('dis-ease') as a teacher

Doctor/patient relationship management

Dowsing (medical & Vega)

Dream-work

Drugs & side effects (management of)

EMDR (for post-traumatic stress)

Emotions management (getting rid of 'baggage' - see Time Line Therapy)
Anger, Sadness, Fear, Hurt, Guilt, Conflict, Shame

Energy/stamina management (emotional, physical and spiritual)

Environment management - noise, pollution, radiation, smoke/exhaust fumes, relationships.

Exercise & fitness: Aerobic conditioning, cycling, dancing, golf, running, swimming, progressive walking, yoga

Expectations (from others):unrealistically high/low?

Expressiveness (ability to be expressive?)

Enemas (coffee and other)

Excesses/over-indulgences (all areas)

Failure/set-backs (reframing - changing the meaning of, dealing with)

Fairness

Family dynamics and therapy

Family/important other - their need to help/for help

Fear(s) (current)

Fears (about the future)

Feedback to medical advisers (positive/negative formal/informal)

Feeling feelings (noting you have them)

Feelings (capacity to share)

Fellowship

Fighting attitude/ability (cultivation of)

Fighting the 'guilt trippers'

Fighting the 'bad-news-mongers'

Food combining (menu planning and cooking)
Frustration assessment and management
Financial planning & assistance (source of stress)
Firm resolution/commitment to live (objections?)
Fixer attitude (letting go of yours?)
Forgiveness (for-*giveness*) training
Friends (keeping them, allowing them to be themselves, dealing with their 'help' etc)
Frustration management
Future (sense of?)
Gem therapy
Getting love & attention without being sick!
Giving and altruism (as a source of healing)
Grief (past, unresolved, and now)
Groups (see support groups)
Group therapy
Healing: Hands-on, absent, religious, spiritual, self, self activation of, other?
Helplessness management
Herbal therapy
Hexes & beliefs from the past ("You'll die before you're 30....") (have you ever been given bad news about your health?)
Hobbies (fun/leisure)
Holiday therapy (referrals & resources abroad))
Homeopathy (complex, traditional etc.)
Honesty
Hopelessness
Hospice (attitude towards and use of support)
Hydrotherapy
Hypertension (biofeedback device)
Hypnotherapy
Information (see knowledge: too much/little?)
Inspirational people/role models (finding them)
Intentions: (stating and communicating them to self, to the unconscious & to others)
Interests (new)
Intimacy (sexual and non-sexual)
Ions (-) therapy: The sea, Ioniser
Insurance (life, medical etc.)
Journalling (Pennebaker) as a form of expression
Kinesiology
Knowledge/education/information/reaction (about the condition)
Knowledge/education/reaction (about the prognosis)
Knowledge/education (about your body and its capabilities)
Knowledge/education/reaction (choices in treatment?)
Language (inner dialogue/pain in the ....)
Laughter therapy (Norman Cousins etc)
Letting go (of life, things, abilities, people, sexuality, driving, independence, power, concentration, memory
Lifestyle change (total and absolute!)
Life direction (sense of) & planning (20 years)
Life purpose (a reason for living?)
Light therapy (full spectrum, etc.)
Loneliness
Love/loving-kindness (giving/receiving?)
Lymph drainage
Magnet therapy
Manipulation (sense of by other /of others)
Marriage conflicts (re-solution of)
Massage: Ki/Aromatherapy/Other
Mastication (optimum feeding of the body - the mouth is part of the digestive system!)
Megavitamin therapy (mixed evidence)
Metamorphic technique

Mayr Cure detoxification
Medical tests/feedback/purpose
Medical carer - attitude of/communication with? - empowering/disempowering?
Medics (assessment/feedback sheets)
Medication (empowering/boosting yours through mindfulness/visualisation/self-hypnosis)
Meditation:- Benson, religious, TM, Buddhist (Mindfulness/Sati/Metabavna
Memory (problems with/loss of...)
Mineral therapy
Mirror work
Misinformation (managing)
Mothering / smothering! - dealing with
Motivation management (self & others) "How do I keep going, keep on track?"
Money (perspective on) - "How will I survive?"
Museum of personal history (leaving your emotional baggage there!)
Naturopathy
Nausea management (self-hypnosis etc.)
Negativity (habitual) management of ....
Newness - hair styles, clothes, getting away from 'dirty'
Nightmares (resolving of...)
NLP
Normality (trying to keep a sense of .....)
Nutrition (optimum)
Obsessions (dealing with ....)
Occult
Opening self ('one' point)
Openness (traditional conditioning against)
Optimum feeding
Osteopathy
Others (how will they *now* perceive me?)
Others (how we treat them as a model/metaphor of self-treatment)
Out-look (sense of the future?)
Oxygen Therapy (HBO)
Ozone therapy
Pain management (surfing, strategies & integration of)
Panic attacks (strategy for ....)
Past-life therapy (for redefining dying)
Peace-fullness
Peacemakers (find them)
Permission (giving self permission to die or to 'let go'... but only when appropriate!)
Personality trait management & cultivation (Type 'A', 'B', 'C')
Pet therapy
Plant therapy
Plan (recovery) and a battle plan facilitator
Placebo harnessing (letting go of unuseful cynicism/scepticism)
Playfulness training (line-dancing, doing daft - but safe - things etc.)
Planning for/creating optimum healing environments
Positiveness training
Positive emotion therapy
Posture (external statement of inner state)
Practices (what you do <u>every</u> day is what counts!)
Prayer/religion
Property (concerns about worldly goods)

Prioritisation/Balance: life, relationships, occupation, personal, family, health, spiritual, money, time management

Privacy (access to.....)
Piscine medicine
Psychic surgery
Psycho-drama
Psycho-analysis
Purposefulness (purpose-fullness!)
Persuading family/friends to allow you (the patient) to do things
Pyramidology
Radionics
Qi Gong
Raising your sights (where do you go now?) - seeking the outrageous
Rebirthing
Recreation (re-creation)
Reflexology
Remission (in search of re-mission or new start)
Resentment management (too big a price tag!)
Respect (for self & for others)
Responsibilities (legal, financial, emotional, relationship etc.,) ability to continue them or let them go?
Reiki therapy
Reinforcement from others
Relationship (reviewing yours...)
Relaxation training (progressive/Jacobson)
Relics (religious)
Responsibility training - my responsibilities & roles? Who am I reporting to?
Restlessness/agitation/concentration (or lack of)
Retreats (re-treat & solitude)
Rolfing
Rules & rights (communications in the family)
Secrets resolution (letting go of deep, dark....)
Secondary gain from your illness?
Security/insecurity
Self-abusive behaviour, (assessment of....)
Self-expectations (unrealistically high/low)
Self-hypnosis & self-programming. You are already doing it; why not do it intentionally?
Self-image/self-esteem
Self-knowledge evolution
Self-ishness training
Seminars/information (about your condition)
Sex/sexuality (continuance of, communicating your needs to self, partner, doctor)
Shamanism
Shiatsu
Shrine visitation (Lourdes etc.)
Side effects of treatment (management of...)
Simontons' program
Sleeping/resting - duration and quality, insomnia management
Sound therapy
Substance cessation (including chocolate, junk-food)
Spiritual self (accessing of)
Stopping smoking
Stopping alcohol
Stress assessment & management
Support systems (personal)
Support/help (ability to ask for)
Support/help (ability to accept)
Support/help (ability to give)
Support groups (availability, role, frequency etc.)
Suicide
Sunlight
Talk therapies (to talk or not to talk?)

Talk Therapies (cont'd)

Chatting: with friends
Complementary programme management & recovery planning:
Health crisis counselling
Dreamwork
Grieving / bereavement (people, youth, health etc.)
Hypnotherapy
Internal dialogue
NLP
Psychoanalysis
Time Line Therapy

Teflon attitude (dealing with others' negativity)
Therapeutic touch
Tiredness management
Time management (long hours/overworking/ under-working)
Time (changing the meaning of ....)
Tissue salts
TCM (Traditional Chinese Medicine)
Togetherness
Touching/being touched
Unconditional positive regard therapy
Understanding (towards self)
Unemployment (dealing with .....)
Usefulness/uselessness (sense of...)
Values assessment & conflicts
Vanity (its OK!)
Vega Testing
Visualisation/guided imagery
Vitamin therapy - oral - foodstuffs, IV etc.
Water selection and intake (volume, frequency and drinking method)
Wanted (feeling of being....)
Weight management (obesity & under-weight)
Work (future ability to...)
Worthiness (sense of ....)
Worthlessness (sense of ....)
Yoga & gentle progressive exercise

Book References

New Choices in Natural Healing, 1995, Rodale Press, Prevention Magazine,
ISBN 0-87596-257-2
(1,800 of the best self-help help approaches from the world of Alternative Medicine)
ISBN 0-9636334-3-0
(1,200 page guide to Alternative Medicine)
Alternative Medicine, the Definitive Guide, 1994, Future Medicine Publishing,

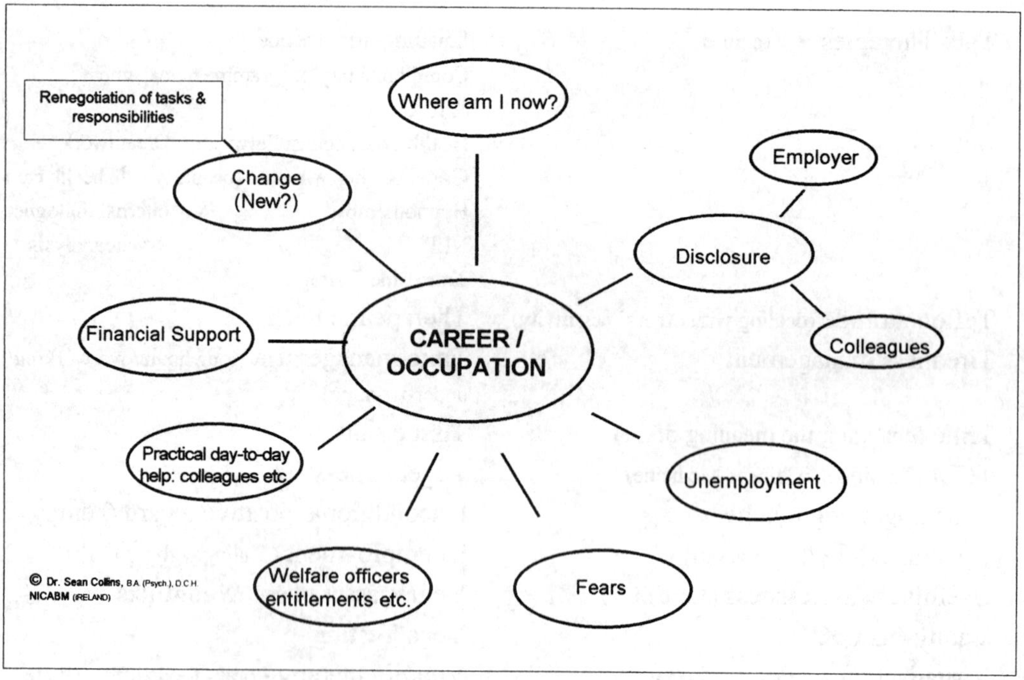

19. **Career/Occupation**: *Aspects of* ***illness and career*** *for consideration*

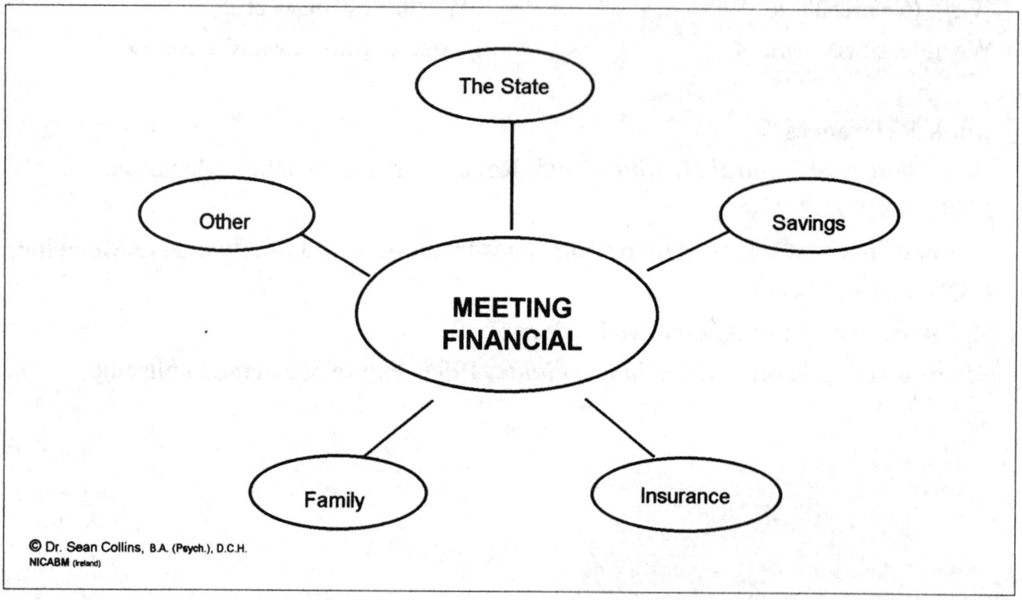

20. **Meeting Financial Needs:** *Sources of funding: start strategising now!*

Booklist

Cancer

Frahm, Anne, (1992). *A Cancer Battle Plan.* Colorado Springs, CO: Pinon Press. ISBN 0-89109-690-6

Lerner, Michael, (1994). *Choices in Healing*, Cambridge, Massachusetts: MIT Press. ISBN 0-262-12180-8

*Spiegel, David, M.D., (1993). *Living Beyond Limits*, New York: Times Books. ISBN 0-09-178641-X

Temoshok, Lydia, Ph.D. & Dreher, Henry, (1993). *The Type C Connection.* New York: Penguin. ISBN 0-452-27082-0

Heart

*Ornish, Dean, M.D., (1990). *Dr. Dean Ornishes Programme for Reversing Heart Disease.* New York: Century. ISBN 0-7126-4896-8 hb 0-7126-5011-3 pb

Whittaker, Julian, M.D., (1985). *Reversing Heart Disease.* New York: Warner. ISBN 0-446-38548-4 pb , 0-446-38549-2 pb

General

Benson, Herbert, M.D., (1996), *Timeless Healing.* Simon & Schuster. ISBN 0-684-81782-9

*Benson, Herbert, M.D., (1992). *The Wellness Book*. New York: Simon & Schuster. ISBN 0-671-797-50-6

Borysenko, Joan, PhD., (1994), *The Power of the Mind to Heal.* Enfield: Grove Publications. ISBN 1-870845-14-5

*Brigham, Deirdre Davis, (1994), *Imagery for Getting Well, Clinical Applications of Behavioural Medicine.* New York: Norton. ISBN 0-393-70169-7

Chopra, Deepack, M.D., 1987, *Creating Health*, Grafton, London, ISBN 0-586-20101-7

Cousins, Norman, (1979). *Anatomy of an illness.* New York: Norton.

* Cousins Norman, (1989). *Head First, The Biology of Hope.* New York: Dutton.

Goleman, Daniel, PhD., (1996). *Emotional Intelligence.* London: Bloomsbury. ISBN 0-7475-2622-2

Goleman, Daniel, PhD., (1993). *Mind Body Medicine.* New York: Consumer Report Books. ISBN 0-89043-580-4

Martin, Paul, (1997). *The Sickening Mind*, Harper Collins: ISBN 0-00-255683-9

Robbins, Anthony, (1992), *Awaken the Giant Within.* London: Simon & Schuster. ISBN 0-671-71188-1

*Weil, Andrew, M.D., (1995). *Spontaneous Healing.* UK: Little, Brown & Co. ISBN 0-316-87611-9

Books marked with a * are highly recommended

Contacts and Organisations

The Irish Cancer Society
5 Northumberland Road
Dublin 4
Tel: 01 668 1855
Freefone: 1800 200 700

Irish Heart Foundation
4 Clyde Road
Dublin 4
Tel: 01 668 5001

The Irish Hospice Foundation
9 Fitzwilliam Place
Dublin 2
Tel: 01 676 5599

Irish Yoga Assocation
Harold's Cross
Dublin 6W
Tel: 01 492 9213

The Irish Institute of Counselling & Hypnotherapy
118 Stillorgan Road
Dublin 4
Tel: 01 260 0118

Dublin Meditation Centre
2 East Essex Street
Temple Bar,
Dublin 2
Tel: 01 671 3187

The Samaritans
112 Marlborough Street
Dublin 1
Tel: 01 872 7700
Callsave: 1850 609 090

Irish Association for Counselling
8 Cumberland Street
Dunlaoghaire
Co. Dublin
Tel: 01 230 0061

Dublin AIDS Alliance
53 Parnell Square West
Dublin 1
Tel: 01 873 3799

IICH and NICABM organise periodic workshops and seminars, in Dublin, on the concepts described in this book. To receive information about these, please telephone IICH at: (01) 260 0118

Biographical Information

Dr Sean Collins is a psychotherapist in private practice in Dublin, specialising in stress-related conditions and also in clinical applications of behavioural medicine.

Educated in Scoil Mhuire (CBS), Marino, Belvedere College (S.J.) and University College, Dublin, he holds bachelor degrees in both psychology and clinical hypnotherapy and, in 1990, earned his earned his doctorate in Clinical Hypnotherapy. He is a Master Practitioner in NeuroLinguistic Programming (NLP), certified by the Society of NLP, and also certified as a Master Practitioner in TimeLine Therapy. In addition, he holds certification in adjunctive therapies including Mayr Cure and Vega BioKinesiology.

Currently, he lectures in clinical applications of Ericksonian hypnosis and behavioural medicine and is working on research for a PhD in Psychoneuroimmunology (PNI) through Greenwich University.

Publications (Books):

Skills for Combating Exam Stress (1992). Dublin: Ardagh.
Skills for Living (1994). Dublin: Ardagh.

Publications (Reports & Studies):

*The Irish Stress Personality (*1993)
(A study of stress in Ireland and the Irish stress personality)

Exam Stress in Ireland (1994)
(A pilot study of exam stress)

National Study of Performance Anxiety (1995)
(A study of 6,500 secondary students and the impact of anxiety on performance)

Fighting Back - The St Michael's Project (1996)
(A pilot research project using behavioural change in fighting back against serious illness)

Epilogue
(Personal)

Intensive care... “Sean, the operation’s over...” Hey, I'm alive! Three days later: standing in my room in the dawn light, practising some gentle Qi Gong exercises... God, it’s good to be alive... to be back in charge of my life! Three weeks post-op: climbing the hundred steps in Dalkey Quarry... an achievement! ...walking three-quarters of Dun Laoghaire pier... another achievement! ...reintroducing my programme... asserting my right to live .....

Month 1: It’s good to be alive!

Month 2: Everything hurts and aches.

Month 3: I guess I'm quite depressed... I'm a psychotherapist, a professional? Professionals don't get depressed... or do they? Why did this happen to me? Was all my fighting-back work a waste of time? Was I going to die anyway?

Month 4: I'm back to normal... and even better!

Sean Collins, Sept. 1997